DAVID
AND
DAVID'S SON

DAVID

AND

DAVID'S SON

13 MEDITATIONS ON SUCCESS AND FAILURE

BY TIM STAFFORD

Franklin Park Press

Copyright © 2021 Tim Stafford

ISBN 979-8-7369-9028-3

Visit the author's website at timstafford.wordpress.com

INTRODUCTION TO SUCCESS AND FAILURE

I'm a very competitive person, though I've spent my life pretending not to be. I hate to lose—hate it!—but I try to act like it doesn't bother me. That's how I was raised—not to be a sore loser, not to push yourself forward, not to brag. Act like you care, but not too much.

My competitiveness fights to get out.

When I was in elementary school, I nearly always got As on my report card. I took pride in that, but I was bedeviled by the "soft" part of the report card—the columns devoted to personal behavior. Very often I found check marks by "needs improvement." My teachers were distressed by how often I "lost it" at playground games. I cried when I was defeated, tears of rage and grief. I didn't want to act that way—in fact, I despised myself for it—but I couldn't help it. The pain went too deep.

When I got older, I learned not to cry when I lost. I never learned to stop hurting.

"Seek first the kingdom of God," Jesus said. I believe in that 100%. And yet, I respond to other incentives: money, fame, prizes, accolades, positions, financial security, beautiful home, loving spouse. We all do. It's part of the human condition. If you are going to live a good life, you have to figure out how to work with this raw material.

My drive for success helps me, for sure. It gets me out of bed in the morning and keeps me going even when I'm tempted to quit. The desire to succeed pushes me to do my best. It can also distort. You act out the thrill of victory in ways that lead to your downfall. ("Pride goes before destruction," as Proverbs would have it.) You let frustration over failure push you into a bad reaction. (The person who gets a bad work evaluation angrily quits the job.)

Recently, a highly successful business consultant told me that for decades he's kept a chart above his desk of every failure he's experienced. He makes himself write them down and he keeps them before his eyes. He knows he too easily falls into the trap of doing what he knows is wrong or stupid in order to gain success. The chart reminds him of the dangers. We all hope for success, and we also dread failure. But we need to guard our souls, which can be eaten alive.

* *

That brings me to David, a man of extreme success and devastating failure. Everybody knows a couple of colorful stories: David and Goliath, David and Bathsheba. There's a lot more. His story is told in more detail than any other personality in the Bible, with the possible exception of Jesus. It begins when he is a young man, probably a teenager, and carries on all the way to his death as a very old man. We know a lot about David, though interestingly enough, the historian who recorded his life makes almost no editorial comment. Hardly ever are we told whether he is doing the right thing or the wrong. We get the facts. And what facts they are.

David saved his people from annihilation—eliminated from history (as were all the rival nations of his time—where can you find a Gittite? An Amorite?). Israel under David's leadership turned the corner from oblivion, becoming a small but reasonably prosperous independent nation-state. David was the crucial player, the king who gave Israel its survival and its identity. He was the savior.

His dramatic successes make a long list: victory in single combat, prowess in leading the army and then a militia of outlaws, political success in uniting fractious tribes, a close and intimate relationship with God, survival from a murderous king. And on the tragic side: moral failure in a midlife crisis, parenting failure when children literally rape and murder each other, political failure when his son leads a successful palace coup against him.

I can't think of a better reference point for success and failure than David. He climbed the heights, and he plumbed the depths. He did it in company with God. Every move is recorded in his prayers—the terrifying, vertigo-inducing lows as well as the intoxicating highs.

Jesus scaled equally intoxicating heights and fell into even deeper canyons. He was called the "Son of David." That has to do with ancestry—the Messiah was supposed to come from David's royal line—but something more, too. Both he and David are characters in the story of God setting a broken world right. They both are great kings, leading their people to victory. Jesus followed in David's footsteps and went beyond, far beyond. He completed David's story. It only has value, ultimately, in the light of Jesus.

We can learn a lot from David, his failures as well as his successes, but what we learn most of all is that we need to get to Jesus. While King David won glory on the battlefield but ultimately came to a humiliating death, King Jesus came to victory *through* humiliation and death. Jesus shows us the way beyond success and failure.

* *

I mentioned that most people know just a couple of incidents in David's life. Even those stories—the fight with Goliath, the adultery with Bathsheba—are known mainly in the simplified Children's Story Bible version.

There's much more to learn about David, and I have to warn you: you may not like what you find. If you look forward to communing with "a man after God's own heart," a wily desert warrior who combined passionate love for God with sterling leadership—well, you'll find it. But you'll also find a man who can be bewilderingly violent, whose politics appear deeply cynical, whose treatment of women is abhorrent, whose parenting is gutless, and who has few friends or none. Eugene Peterson wrote of David, "As an instance of humanity in himself, he isn't much. He has little wisdom to pass on to us on how to live successfully. He was an unfortunate parent and an unfaithful husband. From a purely historical point of view he was a barbaric chieftain with a talent for poetry." (*Leap Over a Wall*, p. 5)

I recently had dinner with a friend who was rereading David's stories in the Bible. He said he was taken aback by it—he didn't like David at all.

Actually, you risk that reaction reading any part of the Old Testament. God's people have their good moments, but they have more awful moments. All through the Old Testament you'll find horrifying violence, ghastly political leadership, abysmal misogyny, and miserable family life. That's not the whole story, but it's a lot of it. God's chosen people are not presented as the best of the best. They grumble when things don't go their way; they aren't grateful when things do. They consistently forget God until they are in deep, deep trouble.

The point is, God saves sinners. If we weren't sick unto death, God wouldn't need to send a doctor.

New York Times columnist Ross Douthat wrote a great Christmas column about the genealogy of Jesus offered up in Matthew's gospel. Douthat makes the point that this list of Jesus' antecedents (including David) is not composed of saints and heroes. Rather, "in claiming the divine is entering the world through this line of 'murderers, cheats, cowards, adulterers and liars,' Matthew... is simply picking up what his own people, the Jewish people, already said about themselves: *We're the chosen people of the one true God, and to prove it to you here's a long story about how awful and promiscuous and murderous and fallible we are, how terrible our leaders often turned out to be, and how we deserved every exile and punishment we received.*"

I'm learning that the awfulness of God's people is not a bug; it's a feature. The Bible's story is not about good people who love and serve God—it's about struggling people, flawed people, messed-up people. God sent Jesus to save such people, and what's more, it's such people God chooses as his instruments to change the world. Because guess what, that's the kind of people who populate the world.

David's life invites us to look deeply into a flawed man—one who did truly love God, and whom God chose to save his people from destruction—but also one who experienced awful failure in every possible way, often because of his own moral weakness. *This* is the man after God's own heart. *This* is the epitome of God's work with imperfect human beings.

The story of David's life invites us to look deeply into ourselves. Much of what we discover may feel embarrassing and wretched. But none of it is so to God, who knows exactly who we are already. Furthermore, none of it is new. Long, long ago, David lived it all in neon. It is all written down in the Bible: shame and honor, envy and triumph.

QUESTION FOR MEDITATION

What does success look like for you? What about failure?

1 Samuel 16:1–13

1. CHOSEN

An ordinary human being meanders along, expecting nothing, unaware that the world is about to pluck her out of obscurity. Suddenly it happens. The light shines laser-bright on a single face. Movie star Jennifer Lawrence was a 14-year-old Kentuckian on vacation in New York City when a talent scout spotted her wandering around Union Square. One moment, she was a run-of-the-mill teenager. The next, a woman who can stop traffic just by walking down the street.

At one time, Hollywood was fascinated by such discoveries. The old movie studios of Lauren Bacall and Humphrey Bogart told stories about stars discovered, just by chance, while they worked at a soda fountain or swam on the high school swim team. The stories suggested it could happen to anyone at any time. It could happen to you!

What makes the discovery so interesting is the surprise. There's no plan. There's not even hope. Destiny comes calling, without announcing itself.

So, imagine David. How old is he? Sixteen? Fourteen? He's the youngest in a big family, which means he rarely gets noticed. His clothes are hand-me-downs from his big brothers, and he is assigned the job nobody else wants: watching the sheep. Out under the sun all day, every day, he fills his time the way teenage boys often do—by throwing rocks at trees, and by playing guitar. Actually, David plays a lyre, writing songs and singing them to himself. He has plenty of time for it. The life of a shepherd is 99% boredom and 1% sheer panic, the latter when a bear or a lion appears out of the brush, moving impossibly fast after the sheep.

David wants to be ready for predators, so he drills with his sling, over and over again, day after day after day, becoming a deadly shot. He has nothing better to do.

David does successfully ward off some predators. Not that anybody in the family pays much attention. He's doing his (lowly) job, and you don't expect praise for that. Besides, none of his family is around to see. It's just him and the sheep.

Then, one day, a servant is sent to fetch him. What for? What's going on?

"You know Samuel?"

"Yeah, heard of him. What about him?"

"He's here."

"For what?"

"Dunno. Some kind of feast. They've slaughtered a heifer, and they want you to come."

A feast sounds good. David's diet is limited when he's out with the flock. But Samuel? That's concerning. There's been some kind of falling out between that old man and the king. Nobody talks about it. Voices fall whenever the topic is raised. You can get killed for being on the wrong side of a quarrel in this time and place. In the background are always the Philistine raiders, who can appear without warning and slaughter anybody they catch out in the open. Israelites need King Saul to lead the army and defend against these raiders. Anybody on Saul's enemies list is an unwelcome guest. David has an idea that Samuel is on that list.

Leaving the sheep with the servant, David hustles back home. He's curious. He's hungry. After spending so many days with the sheep, he's eager to see his family. His seven brothers don't have much time for him, but he looks up to them. Literally. Some of them are half a head taller than he.

When David bursts on the scene, it hardly seems like the feast he expected. There's meat on the fire, but his brothers barely say hello to him. Nobody looks happy. The oldest, Eliab, is slouched against a tree, talking to nobody, a scowl on his face. David knows better than to ask what's the matter. Stopping just inside the clearing, he waits for someone to speak to him.

His father gestures for him to approach. He's seated near the fire, on his haunches next to an old, old man whom David has never seen before.

Is this Samuel? Sun-bronzed and gray-haired, he wears a fine patina of sweat and dust on his face. He must have come a long way.

"This is the one," David's father says to the stranger, not even bothering to greet David.

The old man lurches to his feet. He fumbles inside his robe, dust pluming visibly from the cloth, until he finds a leather strap. Never taking his hungry eyes off David, he pulls on the strap, producing a small vial.

"Come here," Samuel says. Hesitantly, David approaches, wondering what the old man will do.

Samuel unstops the vial and pours a dollop of liquid into his hand. David is so close he can smell it. Sharp, peppery olive oil. Before he can shift his gaze away from the hand and into the old man's eyes, that hand has swung up to David's head and clamped on it, rubbing the oil into his hair. Now Samuel takes the vial and pours more, directly onto David's scalp. Oil is running down behind David's ear. It drips between his eyes and down the tip of his nose, catching his lips.

Though he has no idea what this means, David feels lighter, freer. Fear has disappeared. He feels almost giddy. For an instant, he glances at his father, but Jesse's face is inscrutable.

"What is his name?" Samuel asks.

"David," Jesse says, almost reluctantly.

"He is God's chosen."

Chosen? David slowly grasps the meaning of the oil. Samuel has anointed him.

What can this mean? The youngest son, the one herding sheep, chosen to be king? Something unthinkable is opening before David.

The Bible says that "the Spirit of the Lord came powerfully upon David." What does this mean? I think it means that David wants to sing. Spontaneously, on the spot, he breaks into a rhyme of praise. He begins with a hard clapping rhythm, then starts to rock his body with the tune, then to lift up on his toes, then, finally, to jump and skip as he sings. The family watches as though he were a stranger, but David doesn't care. He is singing praise to the Lord with all his might. He has never felt so full of God.

* *

The moment of discovery. It's not exactly "success," but it opens doors to success. I had one such moment when I first got out of college. I had dreamed of writing books since the third grade. Lots of people do, just as lots of people dream of directing movies or becoming rock stars. Not many of those dreams come true. I knew that. So all through school, I lived on two tracks: dreaming of being a writer, but planning to make a living in a more practical way.

When I finished college, at almost the last minute I threw away practical plans and decided to try to find my fortune as a writer. The dream was strong inside me. Ideally, I would have gone off to a mountain cabin to write the great American novel, but I didn't have any money, so I decided to try to get a job in publishing. I had very little idea how to do this. There was no internet then to enable a search. I knew nobody to call. So, I set off in my parents' aging Nash Rambler, scared half out of my mind. I drove from the West Coast to Chicago, planning to look there first before going on to New York, where most publishing was concentrated.

I never got to New York, because a little Christian publishing house outside Chicago offered me a job. With some trepidation, I took it. It was a small, chaotic business, and I wasn't really comfortable with its style of leadership. However, I could live on the $100 a week that they offered me, and it brought me into a place where they actually published books and magazines.

For the first months, I did whatever drudge work needed doing, often in the cluttered back room. I don't remember feeling impatient for more meaningful activity. I was dazzled to be so close to the making of real books. Nevertheless, I was doing the equivalent of tending sheep.

Then one day I met a skinny, blond man named Bruce Olson. He was rattling around in the office, seemingly without purpose. I learned that he was an independent missionary who lived among indigenous people in the remote jungles of South America, and that he had been flown to our publishing house in order to work with a writer on a memoir. The writer, unfortunately, had not met Olson's expectations. After meeting him, Olson immediately said he couldn't work with him. So now Olson was itching to go back to South America while the publisher tried to find another writer on very short notice.

I wasn't privy to the discussions. All I know is that one day the publisher, a large, breathy man I'll call Biff, approached me to discuss my working with Olson on the book. It was a very contingent opportunity. I would write the first three chapters, Biff said, and they would evaluate them to see whether I could write more.

I don't know how to convey how thunderstruck I was. Just a few months out of college, I would be writing the pages of a real book. How was it possible? I had not seen it coming. I had not planned for it or manipulated it. I had been chosen, not just by the publisher, but somehow by God himself. Through no other imaginable route could I have come so far so quickly.

In the end, I got to write the whole book, which was published (and is still in print) under the name *Bruchko*. However, between the time when the writing was done and the book was published, I took another job, much to Biff's displeasure. As a result, you will not find my name in *Bruchko*. I got no credit, but I didn't much care. What mattered to me was getting to write the book. A world of possibilities had opened to me.

* *

Such a moment comes in almost any story of success. Sometimes it happens after years of hoping. Sometimes it comes—as it came for David—entirely out of the dark.

I remember my daughter, a very unathletic teenager who decided to join the high school track team because of the social opportunities. She wasn't fast or strong and she couldn't jump, so she ended up running distance. Her style was terribly awkward. She ran as though she might at any moment pitch forward and land on her face. I went to her first track meet just hoping, for the sake of her dignity, that she wouldn't come in last.

She improved, and for the league finals the coach assigned her to run the mile in the varsity race. Katie was furious. She cried. She protested. There were some very fast runners in the league, including Julia Stamps, who had won national races. Katie was sure that she would be humiliated, that she would be lapped. Her coach wouldn't let her off.

I missed seeing the race—I had Little League practice, I think. When I showed up late, I asked cautiously how it had gone.

"She came in sixth," I was told. I was stunned, as was everybody who knew anything about it. Sixth in the league was very good, especially for a freshman. Evidently, she had speed that nobody knew. She went on to become a wonderful high school runner, bagging scads of medals and ribbons. But looking back, the best moment of all was that first one. It was unexpected, unpredicted, revelatory.

The moment of discovery: think of barefoot college-dropout, LSD-imbibing Steve Jobs joining up with his high school friend Steve Wozniak and, in a year, producing the Apple II, the first mass-produced personal computer. Think of Winston Churchill, an incredibly vain young man who annoyed almost everybody who met him, suddenly discovering himself (and being discovered by the world) when he escaped from a prisoner of war camp in South Africa. Both Jobs and Churchill would go on to do far greater and more important things, but nothing ever exceeded the surprise and exhilaration of their first great triumph, which came seemingly out of nowhere.

* *

The big question about such moments of discovery is: do they mean anything? Are they just exhilarating memories without enduring significance? Maybe. My daughter's career in high school track has no obvious connection to the rest of her life.

David's discovery, however, is the beginning of a divine plan to save Israel. What's fascinating is that nobody sees what God is doing—nobody.

God had sent Samuel to Bethlehem to anoint a new king. Samuel saw David's tall, strong brother Eliab, the firstborn son, and thought surely this was the person God intended. "But the Lord said to Samuel, 'Do not consider his appearance or his height, for I have rejected him. The Lord does not look at the things people look at. People look at the outward appearance, but the Lord looks at the heart.'" (1 Samuel 16:7)

That's our problem. We judge by externals. But it's not our fault. It's all we have to go on.

Samuel went through all seven brothers, and none of them met God's approval. Only when he asked Jesse whether he had any more sons did Jesse remember David and send for him.

If we could see the scene through God's eyes, we would know from the beginning that David is the chosen one. Samuel has a more limited perspective. He knows he is sent to identify the next king, but he doesn't know who he is looking for. He's groping for the correct answer, unaware that Jesse has a son who isn't present.

David's father, Jesse, is blind in another way. He lives with his sons, but the one God wants, he hasn't even bothered to summon. He sees David as a non-entity. He doesn't know his own children.

David is perhaps the blindest of all. He knows nothing. He's with the sheep, who know as much as he does. There's no foreknowledge or advance understanding of what is going on.

We all see our lives through eyes like these. God knows what he wants to do with us, but we rarely get his plans ahead of time. Like David, we herd our sheep, unaware of the messenger who may be on the way.

The beautiful news embedded in this story is that nobody can count themselves out. You can't say you don't have a chance, that your life is going nowhere. You don't know what discoveries await you. Like David, you can practice your singing and your marksmanship, preparing for something. But what opportunities may come and when, you don't know.

In fact, as the Creator God makes each one of us, and calls us by name, we are *all* chosen—for something. It might be public glory. It might be washing pots in a soup kitchen. David was chosen to be king. What about his brothers? Surely God chose them, too. We can't see around the corner to know what God has in mind for us, but under God, we will have our decisive moment of discovery.

Think about that. You are chosen—chosen first and foremost to be God's child, and part of his family. Furthermore, God is shaping you for a unique purpose. Your calling will be revealed in due time. The messenger may be on the way.

Your job is to watch for him, and to listen carefully so that you hear when God calls you. Your job is to practice your skills and be ready when opportunity knocks. Your job, when your moment of discovery comes, is to praise God with all your heart. You are to let the Spirit of God come on you, as he did with David.

* *

In his book *Outliers*, Malcolm Gladwell says that when people talk about great success, they invariably cite three factors: talent, hard work, and passion. Whether it's a Nobel Prize-winning scientist or a Hall of Fame basketball player, the trio of causation remains. Talent: "From the time she was two years old, she could take apart our alarm clock and put it together again." Hard work: "Nobody ever practiced harder than he did; he was obsessed." Passion: "We all loved painting, but she dreamed of becoming the greatest painter of all time."

Gladwell says when you investigate highly successful people, you always find these three factors. But investigate more deeply and you will find other dynamics that you can't control—the luck of being born in the right place at the right time, the family culture that taught you how to work or how to persuade; the money you inherited that got you into the right school. The story of David's anointing fits in with this perspective. David had talent, passion, and hard work, but he wasn't a self-made man. God chose him; he didn't choose himself.

You can't jack yourself up to be God's chosen instrument. It's not your call. God is the one who calls; you answer. That may be disappointing news for some highly ambitious people. But for most, it should come as a relief. It's not all up to you. You get to take your cues from God himself. He can lead you to success—a success that's right for you.

At the same time, there's a warning lurking in David's story. Saul, the king, was chosen in almost exactly the same way: at God's direction, through Samuel, while utterly blind to any such possibility. Saul, however, failed to live up to his calling. By the time David came into the picture, Saul was already rejected by God.

In Meg Wolitzer's *The Interestings*, she tells the story of a small group of teenagers who discover friendship at a progressive, arts-oriented summer camp. The main character, Jules, can't believe that she has been included in this attractive, talented clique. She feels chosen, and indeed she is. Her inclusion is the best thing that has ever happened to her.

After three summers at camp, however, and four years of college, Jules' desire to be an actress fails to survive in the real world. Meanwhile, two of her best friends from camp go on to be extremely successful in the world of television and drama. Every year, Jules gets a Christmas letter from them, which she makes her husband read aloud. It's a form of self-torture for Jules, because she is so deeply envious, even though she admires and loves the couple. She was chosen to be a member of the group, yes, but being chosen is only a door that opens. What one does inside the door can vary tremendously.

You are chosen and called. But when you hear the call, the story has just begun.

* *

Jesus was often called the Son of David. This isn't simply a matter of bloodlines. It's the idea that the life of David, the great king who saved Israel, is being repeated and multiplied in a new era. By Jesus' time, Israel was living their worst nightmare under Rome, the most powerful and cruel empire in world history. Israel looked for a new David to free them from the misery, just as the original David freed them from Philistine oppression. Nobody knew what the new David would look like or when he would appear, but they were looking for him.

Jesus had a moment of discovery when he appeared before John and asked to be baptized. It's a famous scene, immortalized in thousands of paintings. John drips water over Jesus. The Holy Spirit comes to Jesus in the form of a dove. And words come booming out of the sky: "This is my son, whom I love; with him I am well pleased." (Matthew 3:17)

Jesus' career begins with this moment of discovery. It is somewhat like David's, but it is greater than David's. God's voice, not Samuel's, singles him out. The Holy Spirit lands on Jesus as he did on David, but visibly. So the story begins. It's an opening door.

Jesus is just an ordinary person, as far as the crowd perceives. They are blind to what God is doing. Once chosen, Jesus goes around inviting people to join his upside-down kingdom. Some get what he is offering. Some don't. He invites everybody who will listen. He invites us. Nobody can count themselves out. His calling becomes our calling. We nest our lives inside his. We walk in his steps. Jesus' calling, it turns out, is everybody's calling.

When you read about David's anointing, it appears to be just about him: the heroic figure discovered. Light falls on his face, and on his face alone. He's the role model; he's the hope of Israel; he's the hero. Yet a deeper reading of that story would suggest something different. It's God's story, and David is called into it. God is the role model, the hope, the hero. We are called to be holy like him, and like David only insofar as David lives in God. Centuries after David's time, God will appear among us as Jesus, the epitome of all that David was called to be. Jesus completes David's story.

Calling is not ultimately about finding your true self and becoming the hero. You find your true self by *following*. That's what Saul failed to do. That's what David did, when at his best.

QUESTION FOR REFLECTION

Have you ever experienced a moment when you felt chosen
for something significant? If so, what has happened to that?
If not, is it possible you have missed something God wants for you?

2. CONFIDENCE

I'm a baseball fan, and I often hear this phrase from my Oakland A's broadcasters: "He's pitching with a lot of confidence now." It's an odd statement, if you think of it. They are not exactly saying that the pitcher is throwing the ball harder, or more accurately, or more skillfully. They're referring to body language. The pitcher looks like he's in charge. It appears he expects to get the batter out. He doesn't seem afraid.

In my younger years, I coached a lot of Little League. Among baseball beginners, confidence is written in letters ten feet tall. When a boy or girl gets up to bat, you may not know whether they are going to get a hit, but you certainly know when they won't. *They* know they won't. You can see it. They lack all confidence.

Part of what you see is the outworking of past performance. Success breeds confidence. Failure breeds lack of confidence. If you are well co-ordinated, strong and fast, you'll probably do well and gain athletic confidence. But confidence also breeds more success. If you're not afraid, you're much more likely to persevere when things look tough. You're more likely to go at the game no holds barred, with energy and joy. You're more likely to win.

Nobody doubts that confidence is a very important ingredient in success. The question is: how do you give somebody (yourself?) confidence when they lack it? Pep talks don't necessarily do the trick. How many times have I heard parents encouraging their child from the bleachers? "Come on, Jimmy, you can do it!" I doubt they change what goes on in Jimmy's head.

* *

The oddest thing about David's anointing by Samuel is that it passes by like a quick gust of wind and leaves everything unchanged. David's brothers go off to the army to serve the king. David goes back to the sheep. Apparently, nobody's expectation of David changes. He is still the little brother.

So, David is once again practicing his music and hurling rocks at targets. Anointed by God to be king of Israel, he appears like any other teenage kid with a summer job. Is David disappointed? We never get any sense of that. He is the confidence kid.

Sometimes, your character is formed by deprivation more than nurture. David was the forgotten child, last in line, disregarded. He was left alone, and in solitude he grew up very independent. He drew his identity from within himself, not from his family. Strikingly, he became not merely independent but confident. Judging from the songs he wrote, this was closely wrapped up with his lively, personal relationship with God. Alone with his sheep, he gained a very strong sense of God as his protection, his fortress, his shepherd.

His father sends for him again. This time, when David reaches home, Jesse looks at him with more interest.

"The king sent a messenger," he says to his youngest son. "He wants to see you."

David feels perplexed, excited, and alarmed. "Why?" Has Saul caught wind of his anointing? That could put him in danger.

"Something about music," Jesse says. He has never thought much of the hours David spends playing his lyre, considering them a waste of time. Jesse is surely puzzled as to why King Saul wants to see his youngest son. Can it really be for such a frivolous thing as music?

Nevertheless, Jesse knows an opportunity when he sees it. He loads down a donkey with gifts for the king and sends David off with them. It's not every day that your son gets summoned to appear before royalty.

When David arrives with the gifts, Saul takes a liking to him right away. David is good-looking and cheerful, and his playing can take away Saul's blues. Saul wants him to stay nearby, to make music anytime on request. David soon comes to understand that his music is not just for entertainment. When Saul is mentally stressed, he becomes crazily depressed. David's playing helps restore him.

It seems to be a great opportunity, placing David next to the king in sight of all his generals and counselors. However, it never leads to anything significant. To Saul, David is really just a human jukebox.

Then one day, a deep disturbance ripples through the court. The Philistine army has invaded. This is no raiding party; thousands of enemy soldiers are pouring over the border. Musicians are not needed in this emergency; the nation requires every last warrior to prepare for battle. David is sent home.

So, David becomes a shepherd boy once again. He believes he can fight, but nobody else does.

After some time, David's father sends David to the front lines with provisions for his brothers. He is to deliver the food and find out if his brothers are well, then come straight home.

David arrives with his bundle of food at a propitious moment. The army is lined up on the side of a ridge, looking down into a valley. On the other side of the valley is the Philistine army. Both sides are seething with aggression, lined up close enough to hear each other's taunts. The Israelite army is shouting its wild battle cry, which David hears as he approaches the rear of the encampment. Thrilled, he dumps his provisions with the keeper of supplies and runs to the battle line. He locates his brothers, and just as he starts to ask them how they are doing, a wave of panic runs through the troops. He sees some of the soldiers break and run, as though chased by wasps. Indeed, Goliath has appeared in the valley. Even at a distance, David can see that he is a giant of a man, dressed in battle gear, moving ponderously toward them. The sight of him terrifies the Israelite soldiers.

Goliath stands and taunts the whole line. He demands that they choose their strongest warrior to come into the valley and fight him. It will be a test match; whoever wins will rule.

Nobody moves. David can hardly believe it: not one man steps forward to fight this blasphemous giant. Some of the men standing near David say Saul is promising riches to the man who beats Goliath. He will give his daughter to that man in marriage and grant him a lifetime exemption from government taxes. David overhears this and joins in the chatter. He finds the whole situation incredible. "For who is this uncircumcised

Philistine that he should insult the battle lines of the living God?" Fresh to the battle, full of confidence, David is eager to fight.

David's brother Eliab, the oldest and tallest of the eight brothers, hears David talking and dresses him down. He has never had a high opinion of David, and lately, with that foolish anointing by the old man Samuel and with David's going to serve in the king's court, the kid has gotten a swelled head. Now here he is, not even a soldier, making noises about fighting Goliath. Eliab tells David to shut up.

David brushes him off and keeps on talking. That says a lot about David's confidence. In traditional societies, the oldest brother is an authority figure. Younger siblings don't brush him off. Perhaps David's unusual reaction is the result of being the forgotten brother. He has to stick up for himself because nobody else will.

He talks so much that he makes a stir. Word gets to Saul, who sends for him.

The fact that Saul shows any interest in a secondhand report of an unknown person talking big at the battle front suggests how panicked Saul is. Saul is himself practically a giant. If not as big as Goliath, he is certainly bigger than almost anybody else fighting for Israel. If Israel needs a champion to take on Goliath, it should be Saul. Surely that thought is in the mind of every soldier on the battle line, whether they voice it or not. Saul, however, is terrified. He has no confidence to fight Goliath. So, he sends out generous offers to get somebody else to do the job. Nobody bites—until David.

It must be a letdown for Saul when they usher the volunteer into his tent and he sees that it is just a kid. However, David doesn't think of himself as a kid. Seeing right away how it is with Saul—he has learned to read his moods—he has the chutzpah to reassure Saul that he shouldn't lose heart; he, David, plans to fight the giant.

Bemused, Saul explains to this ignorant man-child that he can't take on a veteran warrior. David responds that he has fought lions and bears, and he will defeat Goliath because "he has defied the armies of the living God." (1 Samuel 17:36)

Saul thinks, "Why not?" He has no other plan to defeat the Philistines. He claps David on the back and dresses him in his armor. After walking around in it, David decides he can't use it; he isn't accustomed to its weight. Instead, wearing street clothes, he shakes Saul's hand and walks back to the battle line. On the way, he picks up several stones and goes out with his sling to face the armored giant.

Goliath has finally gotten his wish—somebody to fight—but he is disappointed to see that it is just a boy. He taunts David. "Come here," he says, "and I'll give your flesh to the birds of the air and the beasts of the field."

As Malcolm Gladwell suggests in his book *David and Goliath*, the key words may be "Come here." Goliath is so weighed down with armor he can barely move. He can't run after David. He can only fight if David comes within range.

David has no intention of coming near Goliath. He has a deadly weapon that is effective from a distance. Goliath may seem invincible, but in reality, he is a sitting duck. Mobility matters greatly in warfare, and Goliath has none. What seem to be his greatest advantages—his size, his heavy armor—actually work against him. Perhaps David knows that Goliath is already all but dead.

As he prepares to use his sling, David pauses to make a speech, in which he gives no credit whatsoever to his superior weaponry or his skill. Rather, he praises his God:

"You come against me with sword and spear and javelin," he shouts to Goliath, "but I come against you in the name of the Lord Almighty, the God of the armies of Israel, whom you have defied. This day the Lord will deliver you into my hands, and I'll strike you down and cut off your head. This very day I will give the carcasses of the Philistine army to the birds and the wild animals, and the whole world will know that there is a God in Israel. All those gathered here will know that it is not by sword or spear that the Lord saves; for the battle is the Lord's, and he will give all of you into our hands." (1 Samuel 17:45–47)

In essence, David says that weaponry doesn't matter; what matters is God. He then proceeds to demonstrate that skill and weaponry help too, centering a rock into Goliath's forehead. Goliath falls face-forward, unconscious, whereupon David grabs Goliath's sword and cuts off his head. He then holds it aloft for all to see.

The Philistines turn and run, shocked by their hero's death. The Israelite army rushes to pursue them.

Stunned by the result, King Saul asks Abner, the head of the army, to find out who the young champion is. Saul should recognize David, since

David and his lyre have been in Saul's court for some time. But evidently, Saul has not bothered to take a good look at David. He has sent him out to die without even troubling to learn his name. Saul is a careless man. Abner brings in the young warrior, with David still holding Goliath's severed head, his clothes grisly with Goliath's blood.

"Whose son are you, young man?" Saul asks mildly.

* *

Without his astonishing confidence, David would never have become Israel's champion—not in a million years. He would have taken his cues from those older and wiser, who were terrified.

Saul sent David out to fight only because a crazily confident David volunteered. Confidence enabled David to respond to Goliath's boasting with incredulous disgust—who is this uncircumcised Philistine?—and confidence encouraged him to skip Saul's bulky armor and go out to fight in comfortable clothes. So confident was David that he paused to give a speech before launching into the fight.

The same confidence irritated his older brother almost too much to bear.

Confidence can be aggravating to others, and it certainly is no guarantee of success. You could read David's confidence as that of a self-absorbed teenager, ignorant of the real world and too arrogant to listen to others telling him what he can't do. His brother thought that, and he wasn't necessarily wrong. Overconfidence can be deadly.

And yet, David had two good reasons for his confidence.

One was practice. He had the ideal weapon to face a slow, low-mobility warrior, and he had undoubtedly spent untold amounts of time practicing. If you hope to be successful, there is no substitute for this combination: the right tools, and the practiced skill to use them. That's as true of marketing as it is of hand-to-hand combat.

In his book *Outliers*, Malcolm Gladwell makes the case that true mastery in any field requires approximately 10,000 hours of disciplined practice. He gives many examples, but perhaps the most compelling involves musicians. Researchers queried violinists at Berlin's elite Academy of Music about their practice habits from the time they first took up the instrument as children. They found a very strong correlation between practice and success. The violinists whom their professors rated "elite" had all become very disciplined at an early stage. By the time they were ready to launch a career in music, they had accumulated 10,000 hours of practice—which is a lot. If you practice four hours a day, five days a week, taking just two weeks' vacation per year, it will take you ten years to accumulate 10,000 hours.

The students rated merely "good" had practiced less—about 8,000 hours. And those who were unlikely to play professionally but whose future lay in teaching—they had practiced 4,000 hours. Most strikingly, there seemed to be no exceptions. Researchers found no "natural" violinists who, because of amazing talent, reached an elite level with, say, merely 5,000 hours of practice. And conversely, they found no violinists who had pounded through 10,000 hours of practice but not made it to the professional ranks. The correlation seemed to be absolute: if you have enough talent to qualify for a top music school, practice leads to success.

("If you have enough talent" is an important caveat. I can't make myself an NBA basketball player just by putting in my 10,000 hours.)

We don't know how many hours David practiced with his sling, but it must have been a lot. Therefore, he approached Goliath with complete—almost arrogant—confidence. He knew what he could do.

* *

The second reason for David's confidence is his belief in God. Such faith is a "soft skill," harder to nail down, but you can't miss it in the biblical account of David's fight with Goliath. What first disgusted David wasn't Goliath's boasting about his size and strength, but his jeering at "the battle lines of the living God." In his pre-fight speech, David told Goliath of his impending doom because "I come against you in the name of the Lord Almighty, the God of the armies of Israel, whom you have defied... for the battle is the Lord's, and he will give all of you [Philistines] into our hands."

David trusts that God will certainly bring him triumph, because his battle is God's battle. Later in life, as we shall see, his confidence in God will be tempered by his awareness of his own failings. At this moment of confrontation with Goliath, however, he has complete confidence. He has heard Goliath speak contemptuously of God. He knows God's cause must prevail. So, he walks into a fearsome situation without a doubt.

In his 2005 Stanford commencement address, Apple Computer founder Steve Jobs told about dropping out of college and, while bumming around, deciding to take a calligraphy class. For no particular reason, he studied the skill of making beautiful script. He also learned all about typography. He then forgot it. It was a useless skill. However, ten years later, while designing the first Macintosh computer, Jobs realized that he could apply what he had learned in that class. "It was the first computer with beautiful typography. If I had never dropped in on that single course in college, the Mac would have never had multiple type-faces or proportionally spaced fonts. And since Windows just copied the Mac, it's likely that no personal computer would have them. If I had never dropped out, I would have never dropped in on this calligraphy class, and personal computers might not have the wonderful typog-raphy that they do. Of course it was impossible to connect the dots looking forward when I was in college. But it was very, very clear looking backward 10 years later."

"...You can't connect the dots looking forward; you can only connect them looking backward. So you have to trust that the dots will somehow connect in your future."

"*Trust that the dots will somehow connect...*" That trust comes easier for those who believe in a loving God who directs the details of our lives. Confidence in God breeds confidence that you have been given the tools and the skills to meet the needs of the moment—that "all the dots connect."

David learned to use the sling because he was protecting sheep—a rather low-status career. Few people would have thought that shep-herding was relevant to fighting a giant—Saul certainly didn't—but David recognized the connection: what can kill a lion can kill a giant. David's is a classic case of transferring skills from one situation to another, of "connecting the dots." He did so with confidence, because he believed the battle he was joining was God's battle.

* *

I remember a conversation I had with a Youth for Christ leader while traveling to a meeting by car. We knew each other slightly because I was working for the Youth for Christ magazine, *Campus Life*, which had its offices in the national headquarters. Gary was a deeply sincere man who was trying to understand me. He recognized that I had no calling to the kind of work that he did—working face-to-face with high school kids—but he struggled to grasp what my ambitions were. I told him I wanted to write. He had evidently never known anybody with such aspirations, and it wasn't clear to him that it was possible to make a career out of it.

"Can you tell me somebody who has succeeded at what you want to do?" Gary asked. "Do you have a role model?"

"Sure," I said. "C.S. Lewis."

I look back at my youthful self with a smile. I am not, emphatically not, sadly not, C.S. Lewis. As a young man, though, I saw no limits in the world of writing. I didn't see why I couldn't be just as good a writer as Lewis, or anybody else whom you might care to name.

I was naïve and overconfident—but my confidence gave me courage to try. I knew that a writing career was a rare and difficult thing, but my confidence made me willing to tackle it.

I had two reasons for my confidence. The great W.H. Auden said of aspiring poets that if they claimed to want to express great and noble ideas, he would counsel them to look for another line of work. But if they said they just wanted to hang around words, they might have a future. "A poet is, before anything else, a person who is passionately in love with language."

I identify with that. I was fascinated by the way sentences sound. I could hear the difference between ordinary writing and exceptional writing, and I always paid attention. I learned fluency by ear. It mattered to me. Like David slinging rocks and writing songs, I practiced all the time in my head.

God also played a role in my confidence. I was raised by parents who believed in submitting all of life to God. To them, pleasing God was all that ultimately mattered. They were very gracious about it—it wasn't a load that they laid on their children or anybody else—but they taught me that following God was always to my benefit. As a result, I prayed to God to guide me when I decided to pursue writing, and I tried to determine what he wanted me to do every step of the way. I wasn't so cocksure as to think I always understood his answer, but I had a deep well of confidence that he would never let me down if I tried sincerely to follow him. That conviction, that the universe is ruled by a kind and caring Lord, gave me a deep internal sense that I couldn't lose. I believed that somehow the dots would connect. Even if everything went wrong, I had confidence that it would come out right, somehow, even if that encompassed failure. Such a theology—for I am describing a theology—breeds confidence.

* *

David and Goliath is a story of youthful confidence. Not only does the shepherd boy defeat the giant, but he saves his country from destruction. The women of Israel sing songs to the army as the soldiers return home:

> "Saul has slain his thousands,
> And David his tens of thousands."

They sing because a shadow has passed over their lives and now they are in the sun again. Their children have gained a reprieve from death or slavery. Their homes will not be burned. They have been saved from rape and the harem. Their men will return from the battlefield and life can begin again.

None of David's psalms speaks specifically of his triumph over Goliath, but any number depict the euphoria of a military victory. These psalms consistently revel in the power of God—and never in purely military power. Not once does David boast about his own abilities, or Israel's. He only boasts in God.

Consider the sheer elation of Psalm 108:

> God has spoken from his sanctuary:
> "In triumph I will parcel out Shechem
> and measure off the Valley of Sukkoth.
> Gilead is mine, Manasseh is mine;
> Ephraim is my helmet,

> Judah is my scepter.
> Moab is my washbasin,
>> on Edom I toss my sandal;
>> over Philistia I shout in triumph."

This is God's triumph; David and Israel don't even appear.

In Psalm 144, David does appear, but the victory belongs to God, entirely:

> Praise be to the Lord my Rock,
>> who trains my hands for war,
>> my fingers for battle.
> He is my loving God and my fortress,
>> my stronghold and my deliverer,
> my shield, in whom I take refuge,
>> who subdues people under me.
>
> ...
>
> I will sing a new song to you, my God;
>> on the ten-stringed lyre I will make music to you,
> to the One who gives victory to kings,
>> who delivers his servant David.

Throughout his turbulent life, David retained this sense that God had control of his life and of his nation's destiny. His victories were God's, and to God belonged the glory. Many leaders will mouth such words, but David seemed really to believe them. God had chosen him. His work was God's work, so it must succeed. He had confidence, because he had confidence in a sovereign and loving God.

* *

David's Son Jesus also had confidence—unfathomable confidence. It permeated everything he did. His most euphoric triumph came when he sent out 72 disciples to go two-by-two through all the villages he would soon visit.

With expectations sky-high, he told them that the harvest waiting for them was plentiful. He sent them out without means of support, sure that everything they needed would be donated as the need appeared. And he gave them his unquestioned backing: "Whoever listens to you listens to me; whoever rejects you rejects me." (Luke 10:16)

One might question this confidence. Was it really true that poor villagers would readily share what they had with strangers? Would they really respond to their message? Would they even take time to listen? One might also question whether the disciples understood Jesus deeply enough to receive his unqualified endorsement. Yet Jesus confidently sent out the 72, and they came back brimming with joy.

Jesus told them their success went deeper than they knew: "I saw Satan fall like lightning from heaven." Then he turned to prayer: "I praise you, Father, Lord of heaven and earth, because you have hidden these things from the wise and learned, and revealed them to little children."

To the 72 disciples he said, "Blessed are the eyes that see what you see. For I tell you that many prophets and kings wanted to see what you see but did not see it, and to hear what you hear but did not hear it." (Luke 10:23–24)

That's confidence: believing that your little movement is the pinnacle of history. Jesus had that kind of confidence, and he passed it on to his disciples. Their confidence is all over the New Testament documents: unconstrained delight in finding out how history is coming together; certainty that whatever difficulties lie ahead—suffering, alienation—the movement is headed for complete triumph in the company of their Lord. This confidence was essential to the sweeping success of the Christian message in the years to come—and right up to our time. Christian confidence depends not merely on belief in God's power, but on the sureness of God's character.

The messengers appeared to be weak: unsophisticated, ordinary people. Their message was strange, "an offense to [our fellow] Jews and foolishness to the Gentiles." But Jesus' followers looked in the face of a powerful empire and its hyper-sophisticated culture and wilted no more than did David facing Goliath. They knew they had the right tools to unlock any door, and they eagerly practiced those tools in their daily life—in family, church, and community. (What tools? The tools of love, which they learned from their Lord.) They also knew that God was for them, and nothing could separate them from his love. They had seen it in Jesus. He had given up his life for them.

Nothing can separate you from the love of Christ Jesus. Those who know that feel confidence.

* *

Confidence remains a tricky thing. It can be arrogant and self-regarding. Those who know the love of Jesus feel confident, but some of them, you can't stand to hear them talk, because they act like they know everything. Overconfidence is destructive. It blunders into impossible situations, it mis-estimates its chances of success, it spoils relationships.

Underconfidence is also destructive. It breeds timidity, and brings progress to a halt. People who are underconfident fail to try difficult things.

What you need on the road to success is confidence based on an accurate assessment of your abilities and God's plans in the face of whatever challenge is before you. The word for this is *humility*. True humility is not humble pie. It does not involve putting yourself down or pretending that you can't do what you know you can. Humility doesn't boast, nor does it cringe. It simply knows what is possible, and sets out to do it. Its confidence is based on practiced skills and trust in God. This is the kind of confidence that you see in David, and in Jesus.

QUESTION FOR REFLECTION

Where do you feel great confidence? What gives it to you?

1 Samuel 18, 21–26

3. JEALOUSY

Before David even washes off Goliath's blood, Saul announces that he, David, isn't going back to the sheep. He is going to stay at the court and take command of elite troops—who cheer when they hear it. (Imagine: experienced troops thrilled to be led by a bright-eyed boy. This may indicate how discouraged they have been.) Saul's son Jonathan, also an experienced fighter, declares his loyalty to David and gives him all his military kit as a sign of his devotion. (Remember, David is a shepherd who doesn't even own a sword.)

Returning home, the army hears the wild chant of rejoicing women:

> Saul has slain his thousands
> And David his tens of thousands.

Only one problem. While everyone else hears in that song an ecstatic celebration of two great warriors, Saul hears a putdown. He is in second place. The demon of jealousy pokes a needle into Saul. It stays under his skin for the rest of his life.

And so it goes. Every success may be perceived by somebody else as a threat or a loss. It's not fair and it's not right, but it's reality. Success produces jealousy. Jealousy sets up rivalries that become bitter and irrational. It's part of the terrain of success and failure.

* *

David is oblivious to how Saul feels. The next day he is playing his lyre, trying to calm Saul, who has fallen into an exhausted depression. The king is in a frenzy, spouting craziness. In a sudden, unprovoked lurch of animosity, Saul goes for David with his spear. Twice David eludes him—thank God he is quick!—until Saul can contain himself.

David has seen Saul act crazy before. He puts the incident behind him and goes about his business.

David has every reason to fear Saul, but he doesn't. Instead, the Bible says that Saul is afraid of David, which makes no sense. Saul is king; he has all the power. But jealousy distorts his mind.

Saul begins plotting to get rid of David. He should be worrying about the Philistines, who are by no means defeated. They continue sending battle groups over Israel's border, springing surprise raids on towns and villages, raping, killing, kidnapping. Saul puts David at the head of the army's response. Not because David is the best captain—though he is. No, because in that position he is likely to get himself killed. What appears as an honor—leading troops—is actually a devious way to do away with him.

It doesn't work. David doesn't die. He is very effective in battle, and his popularity grows. Saul becomes even more jealous. He needs to get David to take more risks, so he offers his daughter Merab in marriage. Saul has already promised a daughter to the man who killed Goliath, but now the offer comes with a condition—that David fight courageously. Saul means to dare David into showing off in battle, running ahead of his troops.

Another of Saul's daughters, Michal, has fallen in love with David. When the marriage to Merab doesn't work out, Saul sends word that Michal is available. He doesn't want money for a dowry; he wants 100 Philistine foreskins.

This is a horrifying, bloody demand, reminiscent of the scalps taken in the American Indian wars of the nineteenth century. Collecting foreskins requires a sexual desecration of the body. (It is also insurance against inflated body counts.) For David to kill 100 Philistines, he will have to take big risks. He might die trying.

David takes the offer. For days, he and his soldiers are out in the field. Saul waits impatiently, squirming with the paradox of hoping that his own army fails and their commander dies. Jealousy breeds bizarre thoughts. Finally, word comes that the troops are approaching. Saul leaves his home to meet them, acting the part of concerned head of state, but secretly longing for word that his rival is dead. Then David comes striding into camp at the head of his troops. The boy has not died. David bows before Saul and proceeds to present him with double the required number of foreskins—200 bloody proofs of death. Saul has no choice but to give Michal away, as he so publicly promised.

Three times 1 Samuel 18 says that Saul was afraid of David. But seven times the chapter reports that David was loved: by two of Saul's children, by all Saul's attendants, and by all the people of Israel and Judah. It galls Saul. David is gaining everything he most desires: God's favor, the love of family, and the spontaneous esteem of the people. Saul's jealousy will undo him—will disturb his inner peace, will fracture his family, will undermine his leadership of the army, and will drive away the very commander he needs. Saul's jealousy is literally insane.

Saul may well suffer from some kind of mental illness. Nevertheless, he seems quite capable of choosing how he treats David. He could welcome David, putting his trust in God, who has chosen him as king. Instead, he chooses to destroy David. He chooses to name him as an enemy, to hate and kill him.

Saul is absolutely in the wrong, but before you condemn him, bear in mind how easy it is to be just like him. It's terrible to feel that you are losing your position and the respect that goes with it. Jealousy leads to anger and then to bitter hatred. It's tough to lose.

* *

A very good friend of mine, whom I will call Ray, was number two in a corporation that was a subsidiary of a much larger corporation. When the CEO of his company retired, Ray applied for the position. Many people thought he would get it; he was well liked in the company and had a long history with its clients. When the results were announced, however, the larger corporation chose to name somebody from outside the industry.

Ray was very disappointed, but he is a good sport and he deeply loved the company, where he had such a long, positive history. So, he made up his mind to be supportive of the new CEO. Ray went to him soon after he arrived at headquarters, promising to be absolutely loyal. He told the new CEO that he wanted him to succeed and would back him all the way. The new CEO responded very favorably, thanked Ray volubly, and assured him that he planned to depend on him. Two weeks later, he called Ray into his office and told him he was letting him go. A security officer escorted Ray to his office, let him gather his personal belongings, relieved him of his keys, and saw him out the front door.

I believe the CEO was jealous. He couldn't stand to work alongside somebody others believed deserved his place. The new CEO fired a number of other executives who were part of the old regime. Determined to put his own stamp on the company, he made some bold moves in the marketplace. In two years, he had done so much damage to the bottom line that he was fired himself. It would take years for the company to recover fully.

It all happened because of demon jealousy, the insecurity of a leader who couldn't work with somebody he considered a rival.

Insecurity creates imaginary enemies and leads to self-destructive acts. Consider these two stories:

Christine Paolilla suffered from a disease that made her lose her hair and wear a wig all through middle school and high school. Some kids bullied her. Her life was wretched.

Then, in her junior year of high school, two "cool" girls at Houston's Clear Lake High School befriended her. They did a makeover that eventually resulted in Paolilla's being voted "most irresistible" by her classmates. Paolilla's two friends were murdered in 2003, shot at point-blank range. Three years later, investigators arrested Paolilla. Detectives believe she was jealous of her benefactors for their beauty and their popularity. They had what she wanted most, so she murdered them. Paolilla is now in prison on a 40-year sentence.

In 2013, Melanie Smith was branded "Britain's Most Evil Woman" after she set fire to her apartment building, killing several residents. Smith had grown jealous of her upstairs neighbor Lee Anna Shiers and her happy relationship with partner Liam Timbrell. Overhearing Shiers and Timbrell having sex one night, Smith became furious and set fire to the baby stroller Shiers had left in the hallway. The fire spread and killed not only Shiers and Timbrell, but Shiers' young son, nephew, and niece, who were all staying with her that night. Smith was sentenced to 30 years in prison.

These are extreme cases, but they make the point that jealousy leads people to act in ways that are decidedly not in their own interest. Most people don't murder their rivals, but they can spread nasty rumors. They can undermine a rival's proposal at work. They can quit a group of friends or complain that they can't work alongside somebody whom they used to enjoy. Relationships are spoiled. Workplaces, churches, and neighborhoods are damaged.

That is the case with Saul's jealousy toward David. It doesn't just hurt David; it damages the nation Saul leads. David is helpless to defend himself. Perhaps that is why David's psalms so often ask God to defend him against people who have made themselves his enemy.

> Vindicate me, LORD,
>   for I have led a blameless life;
> I have trusted in the LORD
>   and have not faltered.
> (Psalm 26:1)

> Vindicate me, LORD, according to my righteousness,
>   according to my integrity, O Most High.
> (Psalm 7:8)

David needs God's vindication because he has no way to vindicate himself.

* *

Out of fear and jealousy, Saul makes repeated attempts to kill David. David narrowly escapes and runs to old man Samuel. When Samuel can't protect him, David returns secretly to Saul's territory and sleeps in the woods for three nights. Hoping to be told it was all a misunderstanding, he furtively contacts Jonathan. But no, Jonathan says, the king has every intention of hunting him down.

Where can David go next? His thoughts must circle wildly in the hour or so that it takes to walk to Nob, a place of worship just three miles south. What can he do? How can he survive? David carries no weapon with which to defend himself. He left home without food. Perhaps, he thinks, a place of worship will provide some protection. When he reaches the shrine, however, the priest recognizes him. "Why are you alone?" he asks, sensing that something is wrong. An army commander never travels without a retinue.

David can't give away his situation or he might be arrested on the spot. He makes up a story about a secret mission and claims he is meeting up with his men at a prearranged spot. "And do you have any bread?" he asks.

The only bread available is the consecrated bread, meant for priests only. David takes it, assuring the priest that his men will not be violating purity rules by eating the sacred bread. (Indeed they will not, being imaginary men.)

David then pushes his luck. "Do you have a weapon? A spear or a sword?" The priest says that the sword of Goliath is stored in the shrine. "Give it to me," David says.

He can't stay another minute. Word of his presence is sure to make its way back to Saul, and he will be pursued. (Indeed, an angry and vindictive Saul will murder the priests at Nob, wiping out the town.)

Alone but now supplied with food and a weapon, David goes where Saul cannot follow: into Philistine country, to Gath, Goliath's hometown. It is an insanely desperate measure, venturing into the very town whose hero he killed. He tries to stay anonymous, but the local warlord's men recognize him. Thinking fast, David begins to act like a madman—drooling, marking little scribbles on the town gates. This makes a kind of sense: only a crazy man would walk alone into the city of the champion he had killed. His act convinces Achish, the warlord, that David is a harmless idiot. Instead of executing him, he allows David to leave.

David makes his way into the wild hill country, sheltering in a cave. There, he is joined by other fugitives: men who have run away from their debts, men who are imbittered or in trouble. His family comes, too. David has inadvertently put them in danger, for Saul in his paranoia will suspect their loyalty. Soon, David has a little militia of 400. He takes his aging parents to the neighboring kingdom of Moab, where his father's grandmother Ruth came from. Then, afraid of detection, he moves again, into the forest.

In the wilderness, David learns leadership of a different kind. He has to weld 400 men—ne'er-do-wells, criminals, complainers—into a unified militia. Everything depends on his decisions: where to hide, how to get food, when to build shelter. David learns lessons that will serve him well leading a nation.

Still jealous, Saul pursues relentlessly. Sometimes David and his men barely escape. Not all the locals are supportive; some report to Saul on David's whereabouts.

During this period, Jonathan locates David and pledges his loyalty once again. However, Jonathan cannot provide tangible help. David keeps moving east, eventually finding his way to the rugged, barren terrain of El-Gedi, overlooking the Dead Sea.

David and Saul have two separate encounters in that region, which reveal much about their rivalry.

First incident: David and his men are hiding in a cave, where they are trapped by Saul's pursuing army. Without realizing they are there, Saul decides to relieve himself in the cave. David's men seethe with excitement. They whisper to David, "This is your moment! God has given Saul to you!" But David won't have it. He is a warrior who kills in battle, but he will not kill the king. Instead, he creeps up and with his sword, cuts off the end of Saul's robe. Then, when Saul is safely out of the cave, David follows him out and calls to him.

"My Lord the King!"

Saul turns, and David bows deeply toward him.

"Why do you listen when men say, 'David is bent on harming you'? This day you have seen with your own eyes how the LORD delivered you into my hands in the cave. Some urged me to kill you, but I spared you; I said, 'I will not lay my hand on my lord, because he is the LORD's anointed.' See, my father, look at this piece of your robe in my hand! I cut off the corner of your robe but did not kill you. See that there is nothing in my hand to indicate that I am guilty of wrongdoing or rebellion. I have not wronged you, but you are hunting me down to take my life. May the LORD judge between you and me. And may the LORD avenge the wrongs you have done to me, but my hand will not touch you." (1 Samuel 24:9–12)

Saul is undone. He weeps. "You are more righteous than I," he says. "You have treated me well, but I have treated you badly." He admits to

David that he will become king, and he asks him to swear not to kill off his descendants.

Then Saul goes home to his comfortable bed, and David goes off into the wilderness again. He doesn't trust Saul. He never will again. But he isn't going to kill him.

Second incident: Saul is still pursuing David, and one night David goes out with a few trusted aides to scout Saul's army. They find Saul's camp and look down on a sleeping army so confident that they have not posted a watch. David asks whether anyone will come with him to sneak into the camp, and Abishai volunteers. They make their way silently in the starlight to Saul's very side. He is dead asleep, as are all the troops; his spear is thrust into the ground near his head. Abishai puts his mouth on David's ear and asks permission to take the spear and kill Saul at a stroke. In a whisper, David refuses. "Don't destroy him! Who can lay a hand on the Lord's anointed and be guiltless? As surely as the Lord lives," David says, "the Lord himself will strike him, or his time will come and he will die, or he will go into battle and perish. But the Lord forbid that I should lay a hand on the Lord's anointed. Now get the spear and water jug that are near his head, and let's go." (1 Samuel 26:9–11)

From high above the camp, David calls out to Abner, the chief of Saul's army, asking why he has not guarded the king. "Where is the king's spear and the water jug that were at his head?"

In the pre-dawn dark, Saul recognizes David's voice. "Is that your voice, my son, David?"

David replies, "Yes it is, my lord the king." And he adds, "Why is my lord pursuing his servant? What have I done, and what wrong am I guilty of?"

Saul answers, "I have sinned. Come back, David my son. Because you considered my life precious today, I will not try to harm you again. Surely I have acted like a fool and have been terribly wrong."

David tells Saul to send a man for his spear and then adds these trenchant words: "The Lord rewards everyone for their righteousness and faithfulness…As surely as I valued your life today, so may the Lord value my life and deliver me from all trouble."

Once again, Saul goes home to his bed, and David remains in the wilderness.

* *

These two incidents are difficult to understand, even for David's own soldiers. The Bible recounts them in such detail because they reveal something very significant about David's character, particularly how he deals with Saul's murderous and fear-stoked jealousy.

It may appear insane that David, a warrior who killed Goliath and many other enemies, will not touch Saul, who has made himself an enemy. Saul is trying to kill David; why won't David kill Saul when he has the chance? It's purely self-defense.

But David is not fighting just to defend himself. He fights for Israel, the nation that God has chosen. Saul is Israel's king, until God removes him. God has not instructed David to remove him.

This is at David's core: he is a loyal Israelite and a loyal commander in Saul's army. Though made desperate by Saul's treatment of him, he will not let it change his basic orientation. He will not attack Saul. He will honor the throne even if he cannot honor the man sitting on it.

The king, he believes, has been chosen by God. In ordinary life, he would never attack the king. It is true that he, too, has been chosen, and by God's choice he will succeed Saul. That timing, however, belongs to God, not David. His calling is to be a loyal Israelite and wait—indeed, to support Saul. He will not allow Saul to deprive him of that calling.

David's behavior reveals a man determined to remain himself, to live by his principles no matter the provocation. In a strange way, David prefigures the Christian martyrs, who were treated with ultimate injustice—tortured and murdered because they would not surrender their faith. We do not remember martyrs only because they died, but because of the way they acted as they were killed. They blessed God. They blessed those who persecuted them. That is who they were, and they were not willing to let their tormentors change them.

The greatest challenge when you are treated unjustly by a rival is to remain who you are. You can easily become somebody you do not want to be.

* *

David's Son Jesus experienced calamitous jealousy from a group known as the Pharisees. They were jealous because they had set their ambitions on being very good people, and yet God seemed to favor Jesus over them. The crowds followed him and ate up his words. God healed people through him, rather than through the Pharisees. The Pharisees wanted that kind of eager adulation from ordinary people, and they certainly wanted to be channels for God's power.

So, jealousy grew. The Pharisees manufactured a trial and turned Jesus over to the occupying army. It was jealousy, as much as anything, that crucified Jesus.

Jesus' response to his persecutors echoes David's. At his rigged trial, Jesus maintained respect for the officials. He might have called on his supporters to strike back, but he didn't. He asked God to forgive the men who were killing him.

That's how you respond to jealousy. You don't hit back. You pray for those who think they are your enemies. You show appropriate respect for their position, trusting that God will redeem your reputation. Undermining or badmouthing them isn't called for. "An eye for an eye" is not your ethic.

What about the other side of jealousy? What about when you're the one who is jealous?

From the first day he saw Jesus, John the Baptist recognized him as God's choice. For a time, the two men carried on parallel ministries, preaching about the kingdom of God and baptizing people. But then, Jesus' ministry began to outgrow John's. This concerned John's followers, who felt jealous on his behalf. Here is John's response:

"A person can receive only what is given them from heaven. You yourselves can testify that I said, 'I am not the Messiah but am sent ahead of him.' The bride belongs to the bridegroom. The friend who attends the bridegroom waits and listens for him, and is full of joy when he hears the bridegroom's voice. That joy is mine, and it is now complete. He must become greater; I must become less." (John 3:27–30)

The first sentence is very important. "A person can receive only what is given them from heaven." Every one of us is given a role to play, though usually—as I noted in David's anointing—we don't know what it is ahead of time. We naturally imagine doing great things, but the "great thing" comes from heaven, not necessarily from our plans or our ambitions. For John, heaven assigned second fiddle.

"The second fiddle," said the great conductor Leonard Bernstein. "I can get plenty of first violinists, but to find someone who can play the second fiddle with enthusiasm—that's a problem. And if we have no second fiddle, we have no harmony."

Charles Spurgeon put it more simply: "It needs more skill than I can tell, to play the second fiddle well."

John displayed that skill. He spoke of his great joy in hearing the bridegroom's voice. "He must become greater; I must become less." We may imagine we hear resignation and sadness in that, but John says otherwise. He took it in joy.

I cannot help wondering how it would have been if Saul had taken John's path, accepting David with joy. Instead, he let jealousy take over his life.

And David? He could have killed Saul and proclaimed himself king. It's very likely he would have succeeded, but at what cost? What would have become of his beloved nation if one king succeeded the other through assassination?

We know the answer to that, because it is the most common succession plan in the world. History offers countless examples of rulers assassinating other rulers in the struggle for power. Israel's calling was different. God was its true ruler; he appointed its kings. David never forgot that.

He also never forgot that his survival depended on God, and on God alone.

> Keep me as the apple of your eye;
>   hide me in the shadow of your wings
> from the wicked who are out to destroy me,
>   from my mortal enemies who surround me.
> (Psalm 17:8, 9)

> The LORD is my light and my salvation—
>   whom shall I fear?
> The LORD is the stronghold of my life—
>   of whom shall I be afraid?
> (Psalm 27:1)

* *

I'm old enough to know that I am not going to reach all my dreams. I'm not going to win the Nobel Prize for literature. I'm pretty sure I won't make the *New York Times* bestseller list. It's all relative, isn't it? No matter how successful you are, you could be more so. The movie stars who won last year's Academy Award want to win this year's and feel a little sorry for themselves when they don't. The billionaire wants to move up on the Forbes list of the world's richest people and pouts when he moves down instead.

Jealousy falls one way or another. If you are successful, others will be jealous of you. If you are not successful, you may be jealous of others who are.

I've experienced both. Occasionally I realize that somebody is actively jealous of me: jealous that I am a successful writer, jealous that I have a happy marriage, jealous that my kids are doing well. It comes as a shock to me. Why would they feel that? My successes aren't exactly grand. And even if they were, what's that to you? You didn't lose anything in the transaction. Jealousy seems inappropriate. I find it disorienting and weird.

But then I sometimes feel jealous of others, particularly my good friends who have done well. I don't want to feel jealous, but I do. That feeling could probably eat me alive if I let it.

Either side of jealousy, you can become somebody you don't recognize. The challenge is to treat it like the weather: a passing event that will not change you in any fundamental way. The challenge is to remain who you are. Like David, who would not allow Saul's jealousy to change him into a king-murderer.

David prayed the psalms, and he passed them down to us so that we could pray them as well. I don't know a better recipe for centering your identity. Because the psalms don't pretend. They speak of how life feels—sometimes rotten and unfair. The psalms contain a whole universe of emotion—they complain, they protest, they howl—but they howl to God. They always come to God. Nobody, but nobody, can help you center your identity like God, because he made you, he knows you, he loves you. There's no reason for jealousy to affect that at all.

QUESTION FOR REFLECTION

Do you have a jealous rival? How do you respond?

1 Samuel 18:1–4; 19:1–17; 20; 23:14–18

4. FRIENDSHIP

For a long time, I thought David's friendship with Jonathan was a big fuss about nothing. So they were great friends! Wonderful! Friends are nice!

That's perhaps a typical male reaction. American men don't have many friends. We may have "buddies" who rib and jostle each other while watching sports, but we don't often speak about deeper things. Doing that could be scarily intimate.

Deep friendship can be especially scarce among ambitious men, because friendships compete for your time. There's always a trade-off with your work.

(I apply this to men, but it's conceivable that women will behave in the same way as more of them gain powerful positions.)

Here's the thing, though: ambitious people sooner or later will need friends. They work long and exhausting hours to see their ambitions fulfilled. They take risks and invest hope in chancy possibilities. The results are often disappointing.

Even success can be disappointing. If you imagined that life would become rich and fulfilling after you reached your goals, you may find yourself disheartened. Money may buy houses, boats, and vacations, but never love. More than a few people have testified that it's lonely at the top; that when they finally "made it to the big house," they found the house empty. If you haven't invested in friendships on the way up, you won't find them after you succeed. You really need friends to help make sense of it all.

* *

So imagine the scene. David walks back from the battle lines, sticky with Goliath's blood, dizzy with praise, happy but disoriented. He hears crowds of women chant his name. Up until this moment, he's been the little brother, the messenger boy, the sheep herder. Just hours earlier, David's own brother reamed him out as an arrogant twerp. Never before has he been the center of such adulation.

In the midst of this frenzied celebration, Jonathan appears. He is older than David, a proven warrior, the king's son, a man among men, and he is staring at David as though starstruck. It is more than admiration. The language of Scripture is extraordinary: "Jonathan's very self became bound up with David's, and Jonathan loved him as himself."

There really is such a thing as love at first sight, and not only in romantic love. Friendship sometimes develops suddenly, helplessly, powerfully. That seems to be the case with David and Jonathan.

The language is so strong that some have speculated about a homoerotic connection. But that is reading our society back into David's. In ancient times, friendship could be described in the most passionate, dramatic terms without any implication of sexual attraction.

The Bible says twice in four verses that Jonathan loved David like he loved his very self, but it says nothing about whether David loved Jonathan back. Jonathan's love is one-sided, as far as we can see. David agrees to make a covenant with Jonathan—some kind of blood-brother oath. Assuming that Jonathan proposes this, it would be strange for David to refuse. Jonathan has everything to offer David; David has almost nothing to offer back. How can the shepherd boy refuse? But one-sided friendships have to grow, or they will die.

* *

Jonathan is in training to succeed his father as king, but now his career plans take a back seat to this new, passionate friendship. He gives David his clothing and his weaponry. We don't have a modern equivalent of this: it would perhaps be like making a new friend and on the spot, making a gift of your car.

This friendship almost immediately smashes up against Saul's jealousy. Saul orders Jonathan to kill his new blood brother. Jonathan instantly makes his choice—to go against his father, the king. He leaks Saul's murderous plans to David and instructs David to hide while he goes to his father to try to change his mind.

Jonathan still believes he can talk rationally to Saul. Wonder of wonders, Saul is won over. His rage diminishes and he swears to Jonathan he will not kill David.

The peace doesn't last, however. Another Philistine raiding party attacks; David leads his company out to drive them off. Such successes trigger Saul's jealousy. Isn't that how it always is? I don't think I'd ever be jealous if my friends and colleagues would stop succeeding.

Saul's mood plunges down once again. The whole house is rattled when they see him in such a state. They call on David to calm Saul with music—the only cure anyone had found. But as David plays, the demon of jealousy comes on Saul, and he goes after David again. His spear misses David and sticks into the mud-and-wattle wall. David runs, out into the night.

Saul orders the head of the palace guard to follow, to watch David's house and kill him when the gates open in the morning. Perhaps Michal, David's wife, peers out and sees Saul's men lurking in the darkness. She knows her father, and (unlike Jonathan) is sure that rationality will never control him. David will be dead in the morning, she tells him, unless he runs now. With her help, he lowers himself from a window and gets away.

David is left desperate. What options does he have? He can't go back to Saul. If he returns to his family home in Bethlehem, he will bring Saul's deadly enmity there.

Only one possible option occurs to David: to go back into the heart of danger, to the one place where nobody expects to see him. Somehow he sneaks into Saul's camp and finds Jonathan. "What have I done?" he asks Jonathan in agony. "What is my crime? How have I wronged your father, that he is trying to kill me?"

Jonathan still can't believe that Saul wants to kill David. Surely his father—who tells him everything—would reveal such a plan!

The one-sided nature of the friendship shows in their conversation. David clearly does not trust Jonathan. Only because he has no other options has he come to him. He pushes Jonathan to the limit. Will he go against his father? Against his own future inheritance?

Jonathan beckons David outside, into the field. Once in the clear, where no one can overhear, he swears before God—a most solemn oath—to sound out his father and tell David what he learns, whether favorable or not. He swears he will not betray his friend.

The conversation grows even more emotional. "May the Lord be with you as he has been with my father," Jonathan says, revealing that he believes David will be king. "But show me unfailing kindness like the Lord's kindness as long as I live, so that I may not be killed, and do not ever cut off your kindness from my family—not even when the Lord has cut off every one of David's enemies from the face of the earth."

He is pleading not to be murdered when David is crowned—a reasonable concern, since killing potential rivals is the normal procedure. Jonathan is acknowledging that he and his father have no future in government. Though they hold the highest positions in Israel, they will lose them. Jonathan is saying good-bye to all that in favor of his friendship with David.

On the spot, Jonathan renews his oath of loyalty to David, and he asks David to do the same to him, "because he loved him as he loved himself." Then they get down to practical business, making a plan by which Jonathan can secretly bring news to David.

* *

In May 1940, with Great Britain newly at war with Germany, Winston Churchill became Prime Minister. One of his first priorities, never publicly stated, was to become close friends with American President Franklin Roosevelt. "No lover ever studied the whims of his mistress as I did those of President Roosevelt," he later recalled. Churchill painted a landscape for Roosevelt, he sang for him, he crafted laudatory notes and agonized when they went unanswered. Churchill had a well-developed ego, but he submerged it to befriend Roosevelt. Over the next five years, the two exchanged nearly 2,000 letters and spent 113 days together, including Christmas and other major holidays.

Though Churchill is remembered as a tempestuous personality, Roosevelt was the more difficult of the pair: outwardly charming, but inwardly vain, cold, and often unfeeling. Churchill was not deterred. He did not pursue Roosevelt for personal reasons. He believed that friendship would cement the alliance of the United States to Great Britain.

During the first years of the war, strong political forces opposed any American involvement. The "America First" movement sponsored huge rallies urging Washington not to side with Britain. Churchill understood that America's course would not be decided on purely rational grounds. He believed that personal friendship would clear the way for Roosevelt to lead America into supporting Britain.

It worked. An extraordinary politician, Roosevelt eased a skittish America onto Britain's side in the war, providing ships and food and tanks and airplanes without which the United Kingdom would have been unable to defend itself.

We need friends because dark times will come. Friendship can bridge the fierce rivalries that ultimately destroy.

The friendship between Jonathan and David bridged two ambitious dynasties—Saul's, the first monarchy in Israel's history, and David's, which would go on to replace Saul's line and carry on for centuries. This would have been a murderous rivalry if Saul had his way. But Jonathan's friendship intervened. In the short run, he saved David's life from Saul's bloody plans, and in the long run, their friendship would preserve what was left of Saul's family after his regime collapsed. For David would not forget Jonathan's friendship. In the civil war that came after Saul and Jonathan's death, David avoided retribution against Jonathan's family. The David-Jonathan friendship became the pattern for reconciliation between the warring factions of Israel.

* *

When Jonathan finally talks to his father about David, Saul swears violently at his son, whom he accuses of siding with David against him. "As long as [David] the son of Jesse lives on this earth, neither you nor your kingdom will be established. Now send someone to bring him to me, for he must die!"

"Why should he be put to death? What has he done?" Jonathan shouts back. With a hideous cry, Saul hurls his spear at Jonathan. Jonathan dodges the spear and leaves.

The next morning, he goes into the country to practice his archery, taking a boy to fetch arrows. When Jonathan tells the boy the arrows he shot are farther away, it is a prearranged signal that David must go farther away because Saul means to kill him.

That is all the communication that is necessary, but it is not enough for Jonathan. He sends the boy home. When he disappears, David comes out of hiding. He bows to Jonathan, his face to the ground. Then he embraces Jonathan. They kiss, weeping—David the more violently of the two. Something has changed. The friendship is no longer one-sided. The independent-minded David now reciprocates the love that Jonathan gives. Overcome with emotion, he can say nothing.

Jonathan says, "Go in peace, for we have sworn friendship with each other in the name of the LORD, saying, 'The LORD is witness between you and me, and between your descendants and my descendants forever.'"

Then David picks up his knapsack and leaves, still a fugitive. They will see each other one more time, years later when David is still hiding in the wilderness, running from an unwavering, relentless Saul. Somehow, Jonathan locates David and offers encouraging words. "Don't be afraid," he tells David. "My father will never lay a hand on you. You will be king, and I will be your number two. Even my father knows this perfectly well."

Soon after, Jonathan lies dead on the battlefield, along with his father. Saul's death liberates David from his fugitive status. But Jonathan's death leaves him without a friend. As far as we know, David never has another. That will cost him very dearly.

Of all the people associated with David, there is not one to whom he can bare his soul, other than Jonathan. His chief general, Joab, follows him to the very end of his reign and is loyal in his own way, but he's never a friend. The Bible describes the military feats of warriors who followed David but says not one word about the emotional support they provide. The prophet Nathan may come closest to true friendship, but when crisis comes, David doesn't say a word to him. In David's most trying moments, we hear nothing of Nathan at all.

Friendship is difficult for those who are in charge. How can you be true friends with subordinates, whose jobs depend on you? Sometimes family members offer a more equal relationship—but David's brothers are never mentioned, and he and his sons are on terrible terms.

It's hard to avoid concluding that David's friendship with Jonathan stood alone. They saw each other only a handful of times over the years, and almost all their encounters were in moments of crisis, when they reached across the void to each other. Through his years leading Israel, David was friendless—which goes some way to explain why he often made a mess of things.

* *

Jesus, David's son, did not neglect friends. He needed them, as we all do. He carefully chose his disciples and traveled with them, talking and working together. Jesus pointedly called them his friends. (John 15:15) Lazarus was a particular friend, and so, evidently, were the sisters Mary and Martha. Jesus was a rabbi and a great man, followed by huge crowds, yet he had the humility to relate as a friend with his co-workers. They loved him not only because of his greatness, but because he cared for them and made himself vulnerable with them.

When he came to Jerusalem, knowingly facing death, Jesus took three of his disciples with him while he prayed about his coming arrest and trial. He told Peter, James, and John, "My soul is overwhelmed with sorrow to the point of death. Stay here and keep watch with me." (Matthew 26:38)

They couldn't do it. While he wrestled with his fate, his friends kept falling asleep. Ultimately, he would face trial and death without support —in a hostile crowd, alone.

None of us has to do that. None of us must face the kind of loneliness that Jesus did. We always have Jesus. He promised that he would never leave us. Plenty of people have found his company precious through very terrible times.

A friendship with Jesus does not come out of nowhere. It takes time. You get to know Jesus by talking to him and by listening to him, by absorbing his thoughts and by teaching yourself to respond to them. Day by day. Night by night. Jesus will be there for you anytime, under any circumstances. But you probably won't go deep with him unless you work on it long before trouble comes.

All friendships require patience and persistence. Maybe they happened without effort when you were 16, but now, when you have a serious job and a family and responsibilities, you must work at it. You must learn to persist even when conversation is awkward. You must have patience to let friendships develop at their own pace. You can't schedule them. The only thing you can schedule is time—to make sure that you give people time. A form of passivity is needed—to let friendship come to you in its own way, and to wait expectantly while it does. A form of activism is needed: to make sure you see people regularly, to make phone calls and write notes when you don't have any agenda but friendship; to pay attention to people and their needs. Fred Rogers of "Mr. Rogers' Neighborhood" kept files on those he hoped would become lasting friends. That may be extreme, but it's definitely not stupid.

You never really know how deep your friendships go until they are tested. Some friendships prove flimsy and unhelpful when you are in trouble. Others surprise you with their resilience and depth. That's what happened between David and Jonathan. David didn't fully reciprocate until his life was on the line. Then he saw Jonathan's dedication, and—in a flash—recognized what Jonathan meant to him. David desperately needed both logistical support and soul care, and he had both through Jonathan. That is why he wept so extravagantly while saying good-bye.

I've never feared for my life as David did, but I remember times of great stress when friends were all I had to hang on to. Times of great loneliness, like when the woman I had fallen deeply in love with showed no romantic interest. Times when I feared public disgrace, like when the business I'd launched seemed destined for bankruptcy. Times when I needed to confess to somebody because a pattern of sin seemed un-breakable. Those were times when I discovered what friends I had, and how much I needed them.

As you get older, friends become harder and harder to gain. Your ambition gets in the way. Your schedule gets in the way.

Don't let them.

QUESTION FOR MEDITATION

What friend is a foundation stone for your life—
when you are on top, and when you are in the dark?

1 Samuel 27, 29–31

5. LOST

I met Tarek in a pizza restaurant in Berlin. He wore a customized T-shirt that he got that day from six German friends who share his birthday. The shirt said "Peace" in Arabic. With his light skin, his short beard, and his stocking cap, Tarek could pass for a German. The truth is, he was a Syrian refugee. He came from an educated, middle-class family in Aleppo. One brother is a dentist; another graduated with a degree in electrical engineering; both parents worked for the Syrian government. Tarek is proud of his Syrian culture, which he sees as creative and welcoming. But "there is no Syria anymore."

He was working in Qatar when the Syrian civil war broke out. He heard news of friends dying or disappearing. The news tunneled into his psyche, distressing him so deeply he could hardly function.

He flew to Turkey, where his parents, his fiancée, and several siblings joined him, fleeing the war. For a time, Tarek produced and sold olive-oil soap in Istanbul. He married his fiancée, who was soon pregnant. Ironically, this was the impetus for him to try to reach Europe. He saw no future for his family in Turkey, where he could not work legally, and he knew they could never return to their home in Syria.

The journey began with a smuggler leading him and four others across the Turkish border into Bulgarian forests. The smuggler disappeared, and the group spent three days wandering, lost, without food or water. Eventually they stumbled on some forest rangers, who called the police. Tarek's group was thrown into prison for two months, under abysmal conditions. "Two women lost babies, and nobody cared." Eventually, thirty refugees went on a hunger strike. Under pressure, the prison authorities let the refugees buy their way out of prison. Tarek got his brother to send him money and was released.

Tarek found another smuggler but was caught and arrested again. (He believes that the smuggler himself called the police.) This time, he was only held for one night, but the temperature dipped far below freezing, and he was given no blanket. One of the other refugees tried to hang himself with his bedsheet. "You feel you should call your family to say goodbye."

Released again, Tarek teamed up with 25 Afghani refugees. They got lost in the forest and were caught by the Serbian border police, who sent them back to Bulgaria. The Bulgarian police beat Tarek and interrogated him, believing that with his good English and his light skin, he must be leading the group. For 24 hours, Tarek says, he was shackled to a wall, standing.

When released, he asked his brother to send money again. This time, he found a reliable smuggler, who—for the price of 5,000 euros—took him on a long, winding journey through Serbia, Croatia, Slovenia, Italy, France, and finally, Germany.

Tarek adjusted quickly to life in Germany. He learned German and within eight months passed a language test that allowed him to apply for work. When I met him, he had a job cleaning apartments and was attending school. He had begun writing a play to be performed by refugees; he showed me a video of his most recent musical performance. "I really respect this country," he told me. "They are not treating us like criminals. I feel safe here. Many people want to help."

Yet he thought constantly of his family. His wife and the son he had never seen remained in Turkey, and he was not confident that he would ever get permission for them to join him in Germany. Three married sisters still lived in Aleppo, their lives at risk from bombs and artillery shells.

Tarek experienced high levels of stress, enough to make him sick. Doctors could give him pills, but they could not cure the disease. He had lost his roots and his culture and his home. New friends could never replace the old ones, some of whom were dead. His future was uncertain. Sometimes he felt like a ghost.

* *

David reaches such a break point after his second encounter with Saul in the wilderness. He has acted nobly (even if his men do not understand why), refusing to kill Saul when he has him in his grip. Despite great pressures to do violence to Saul, David treats him as he believes God requires him to.

Then, after it is over, he breaks. He is tired of running. He cannot imagine ever seeing home again. Sooner or later, he thinks, Saul will catch him and kill him.

Perhaps the anguished words of Psalm 22 are written then:

> My God, my God, why have you forsaken me?
> > Why are you so far from saving me,
> > so far from my cries of anguish?
> My God, I cry out by day, but you do not answer,
> > by night, but I find no rest.
>
> I am a worm and not a man,
> > scorned by everyone, despised by the people.
> All who see me mock me;
> > they hurl insults, shaking their heads.
> "He trusts in the LORD," they say,
> > "let the LORD rescue him.
> Let him deliver him,
> > since he delights in him." (Psalm 22:1–2, 6–8)

David does the unthinkable: he joins the enemy. Leading his 600 men (with their wives and children), he goes to Gath, a Philistine city, intending to offer their services as mercenaries.

David is proposing an action that will certainly appear treasonous. The Philistines are at war with Israel; he offers to fight for them. So much for his future as Israel's king.

David tried to find refuge in Gath before, when he first ran away from Saul. At that time, he went alone, hungry and desperate, hoping that by some stroke of luck he would be able to survive as an anonymous foreigner. The attempt was a total failure; he was very lucky to get away with his life.

This time, David leads a fighting force that can be very useful to Achish, Gath's warlord. They make a bargain. Achish sends David to Ziklag, an outlying town. He gives David and his men rights to live off the spoils of war while raiding other tribes. They get a roof over their heads, a well for drinking water, a place to graze animals. Most importantly, they don't have to run any more.

David tells Achish that they are raiding Israel and some of Israel's friendly neighbors. In fact, they go after tribes who are enemies of both Israel and the Philistines. They kill everyone, women and children included, not as a holy war commanded by God but in order to leave no one who might tell tales. It is a brutal, lying policy that makes no pretense of morality. David thinks he has no choice. It is kill or be killed.

His lies will eventually come to the test, David knows. Achish expects him to fight alongside the Philistines when they go to war against Israel, as they surely will. When Achish puts this to him, David lies without actually lying: "Then you yourself know what your servant will do." Achish thinks he understands what that means. He doesn't.

* *

For a brief period, one year and four months, David and his men stand in this false position. David doesn't have a plan. He carries on, one lie at a time, one day at a time, because he sees no alternative. Saul has made a traitor out of him. He is a hired killer, roaming the earth in search of prey. Women and children are among his victims. He shows no mercy.

Otherwise, he has time to play on his lyre and write songs. In the extensive collection of David's songs are many that speak to a desperate situation and a dark mood:

> Be merciful to me, Lord, for I am in distress;
>> my eyes grow weak with sorrow,
>> my soul and body with grief.
> My life is consumed by anguish
>> and my years by groaning;
> my strength fails because of my affliction,
>> and my bones grow weak.
> Because of all my enemies,

> I am the utter contempt of my neighbors
> and an object of dread to my closest friends—
>   those who see me on the street flee from me.
> I am forgotten as though I were dead;
>   I have become like broken pottery.
>
> Let me not be put to shame, Lord,
>   for I have cried out to you. (31:9–12, 17)

* *

The day comes when David and all his men are summoned to battle headquarters in Gath. If called on to fight Israel, what will David do? Will he really kill his Israelite brothers?

He has run out of options. He can't run and he can't hide. All he can do is to do nothing: to fall in with Achish's men and hope for the best.

As they trudge the rough, dusty road and enter the foothills on Israel's border, David's men join other troops of armed men, all going in the same direction. David's men keep to themselves. A tight-knit band that has fought together for years, they feel their ethnic and religious difference. Nevertheless, they are fighters. The prospect of battle—and booty—excites them. This is not a raid, but an invasion.

The countryside is raw and rocky, crisscrossed by ravines and ridges. David knows this territory; he roamed most of it during his long exile. They are headed north. He begins to speculate as to where the fighting will occur—dreading it.

Then, without warning, the column of troops stops. David hears the sounds of a hellacious argument up ahead. He recognizes Achish's voice; he seems to be quarreling with other Philistines, though David cannot make out their words.

A few minutes later, Achish appears, his face in a frown. He comes straight to David.

"You're a good man," he says. "God knows you've always done just as you said you would. I wanted you fighting with me in this battle. But the generals won't have it. They see you as a dangerous man, and I can't talk them into taking you on. So go back now. Go in peace back to your wives and families in Ziklag. No one will give you trouble if you go peacefully now."

"What have I done to deserve this?" David spits out the words. It isn't hard to act the part of offended warrior. "Why should I be kept from fighting the enemies of my lord the king?"

Achish takes a long, sour look straight into David's eyes. "If I had my way, we would fight together. But the other generals say no. You camp here overnight, and at first light, lead your men back south. I'm sorry, but that's the way it has to be."

* *

The journey home seems more wearisome than the trip out. The men grumble. After a long, weary slog, they get none of the loot they expect from war. It takes them three days to arrive in the vicinity of Ziklag, famished and weary. Their pace picks up as they recognize familiar ground and think of their families. Six hundred men hustle toward home. The air is thick with the dust they stir up.

David senses that something is wrong. Why are no sheep or cattle grazing? Where are the girls fetching water? By now, the buildings of the settlement should be visible, but he sees nothing.

Ahead of him, he hears a terrible cry. It is a man's cry, a deep bass wail of disbelief. The men around David hesitate, then begin to run, their gear rattling and bouncing. David runs with them, racing toward whatever awful thing has caused that cry.

He reaches the town, or what is left of it. Fire has destroyed everything. All the buildings are broken down, their roofs collapsed in blackened beams and heaps of ashes, their walls humbled and shattered. David's men are standing in the street, stunned.

"Where are they?" one sergeant cries.

"Where are they?" Men begin to run again, scattering to their houses, to their stables, to their granaries. All are empty. The assault must have been days ago, for the fires are cold. They find not a creature, living or dead—not a sheep or a goat or a wife or a child.

It takes some minutes for the reality to sink in, and then that same aching cry goes up—not from one voice, but from six hundred. Some roving band has burned the town and kidnapped everyone while their men were marching on their fruitless errand. Their families have been herded off like cattle to be enslaved.

These men know all about loss. They followed David and accepted their status as outcasts in Israel. But now, the last strand of hope has snapped. Without wives and children, they are left entirely alone.

They weep. Some throw themselves on the ground and howl like animals. When David passes by, they look angrily at him. He led them into this. He is responsible for this loss. They ought to kill him.

David knows loss, too. His two wives and children are gone. Nevertheless, some of his soldiers talk of stoning him to death, because he is responsible. He is their leader.

* *

Pause for a moment—let me interrupt this story—to ponder David. Some scholars question whether a real historical David even existed. They suggest that he was invented centuries later to provide a mythic and heroic beginning to the story of Israel—that David is about as real as King Arthur and the Knights of the Round Table.

Such contentions are hard to prove or disprove, but ask yourself this: why would Israel invent *this* story about itself? Its founding monarch was a traitor who fought for the enemy and slaughtered innocent women and children? His band of Merry Men was ready to murder him because he misled them?

Inventing this kind of hero doesn't make much sense. And if the story is factually true, why does Israel *tell* such a story about itself? Couldn't this chapter of David's life be conveniently dropped? Do we have to know the worst about him?

In my career as a journalist, I've heard versions of this question many times. When I've tried to write a profile that paints a Christian leader with failings included, I've received panicky questions. *So and so is such a good man, his work is so important, why do we have to know all the dirt? Can't you drop this material?*

The answer is that David is not the hero of Israel's story. He played his part, good, bad, and ugly, but God is the hero. He saves Israel and makes it great. Nobody takes the place of God.

Furthermore, David's story matches up with real life. The challenges of existence require dealing with the worst kind of fiasco, where you seemingly have no choices but bad ones. Through no fault of his own,

David got squeezed into this situation. He got hounded out of Israel, left with no option but to work for the enemy. He found himself leading a militia of 600 men who came to him because they were desperate. They came of their own free will; he didn't recruit them. They now turn on him because he is in charge, and therefore responsible for everything that goes wrong. Welcome to the joys of leadership.

* *

Who can relate to David's situation? Let me name a few:

An army commander ordered to lead his men in an impossible assault, because his commanding general has a big ego and an unrealistic grasp of the terrain. When the commander protests that the attack will be suicidal, he is told sharply to shut up and obey orders. (It happens.)

A corporate manager told to cut 40% of her staff by next week—not only to identify who should go, but to inform each one of their termination. (It happens.)

A church music director informed by her pastor that the church is changing direction, and she needs to adopt a musical style that she has previously despised. Not only that, she has to explain and justify the change to her musicians. (It happens.)

A community organizer told that the board of his organization, in order to please a major donor, will no longer take controversial stands on community issues. In fact, the organizer is asked to put together an optimistic slide show that completely ignores all the concerns that the organization was built around. (It happens.)

David's situation is worse than any of these. He and all his men have lost their families, and they have no discernible future.

* *

Standing in the smoking ruins of Ziklag, David reaches the bitter end. He is a strong man, a tough man, a warrior. He has tried to keep his soul alive while running from Saul, but Saul pushed him to the breaking point. His last refuge was the unthinkable, becoming a traitor to his people, joining the Philistines, murdering women and children. That has ended in disaster. The Philistines have rejected him, and his own wives and children are lost. His men want to kill him. What next?

A kind of miracle seems to occur right under our eyes. David, the victim, pushed and pulled into actions that are fundamentally abhorrent to him, lying and pretending while leading his men in raids that kill women and children for no reason—that David suddenly catches his breath and finds new life. Scripture puts it simply and enigmatically: "David found strength in the Lord his God." (1 Samuel 30:6)

That could be a cliché, the kind of well-meaning words that drive sufferers into a fury. "Trust God." "It will all work out if you put your faith in God." "God has a reason." For David, however, it means something crucial: he is not alone. God has called him to this moment, and nothing is impossible with God. As David will put it in one of his songs, "With my God I can scale a wall." (Psalm 18:29)

What he actually does is to call for the ephod, the divining instrument used by the priests to channel God's voice. The militia's priest (escaped from the slaughter at Nob) brings it to him. Through the ephod, David asks God whether he should pursue the raiding party. The answer is yes.

Now he has a direction. He and his men leave immediately, moving at maximum speed. They are days late; every minute counts. At the Wadi Besor, David realizes that a third of his force is too exhausted to continue; they are already lagging. Knowing that speed is essential, he leaves them behind.

The trail they follow is cold. David catches a break when they happen on an Egyptian man lying in a field, almost comatose. They might have passed him by, refusing to slow their march for such a lost cause, but David stops to give the man food and water until he can speak. Revived, he tells them that he was a slave to some Amalekite raiders who abandoned him and left him to die when he got sick. He volunteers that the raiders burned Ziklag. David asks whether he can lead them to the raiding party. He says he can, if David will swear not to kill him or turn him over to the Amalekites.

The Egyptian is as good as his word. He leads them to the Amalekites' camp, where the soldiers have stopped for the night and are making no attempt to keep a watch. Rather, they are drunk, making a party of it. David's men fall on them in the dark. It is a complete rout.

Most amazingly, when the sun rises and they take stock, David and his men discover that they have rescued all of the women and children safe and sound. Not one is hurt. The livestock taken in all the Amalekites' raids—not just Ziklag—are booty. David's men are going to make a profit after all. In a moment, they go from utter heartbreak to complete jubilation.

When they get back to the Wadi Besor, some of them taunt those left behind, insisting they will get none of the captured cattle. But David understands the power of magnanimity. In his renewed, God-strengthened self, he insists that everyone get an equal share.

David then goes even further: he sends emissaries to all the major towns in Judah, taking gifts from the captured flocks. David might easily play this less generously. These towns, after all, knuckled under to Saul. If they supported David at all, they did it surreptitiously and inadequately. (After the slaughter at Nob, it was an understandable choice.) David realizes that there is no benefit in replaying old hurts. A sense of hope in God's anointing has returned to him, and he acts like a gracious king. It is the right thing to do, and politically speaking, it is the best thing to do.

David has found strength in God.

* *

Unbroken tells the story of Louis Zamperini, who lived enough drama for three lives. As a young man, he was an Olympic runner who went to Berlin in 1936 and raced before Hitler. A few years later, during WWII, he was flying in a search plane when it crashed into the Pacific Ocean. He and two other crew members were the only survivors out of 11 men. Louis lived an epic 47 days marooned in a rubber raft, living on rainwater and a few small fish. One of his companions died after 33 days. When Zamperini and his remaining comrade drifted into the Marshall Islands, they were captured by a Japanese patrol. Zamperini spent more than two years in a prisoner-of-war camp. There he was tormented and tortured by a fanatical commander nicknamed "the Bird," who singled out Zamperini for special abuse.

After Hiroshima, when the Japanese army surrendered, Zamperini returned to the United States hailed as a hero. He found that his torment had not ended. Recurring memories of the war haunted him, and nightmares regularly interrupted his sleep. He dreamed of the Bird, terrifying dreams in which he tried to strangle his tormentor. Zamperini began to drink. Over time, alcohol came to dominate his life. He fantasized about going back to Japan to find the Bird and murder him.

In just a few years, the adored war hero and Olympic athlete turned into a fanatical drunk, obsessed with revenge.

Zamperini had married soon after the war. He and his wife, Cynthia, had a child. However, alcohol and what would today undoubtedly be diagnosed as PTSD threatened to destroy Zamperini and his family. Cynthia became desperate for help. She found it when a young evangelist named Billy Graham came to Los Angeles, preaching from a huge tent erected near downtown. While listening to Graham, Cynthia found emotional relief in faith. When she urged her husband to attend a meeting, however, he adamantly refused. Eventually, worn down by her urgent pleas, he went to hear Graham, but he walked out angrily when the altar call began.

Cynthia begged him to go again the next night, and after a great deal of resistance, he complied, but on one condition—when the altar call began, he was leaving. He wanted nothing to do with forgiveness. Forgiveness for himself he didn't need, and he wasn't under any circumstances going to forgive his Japanese tormentors.

That night, however, Graham's preaching captivated Zamperini in an unexpected way. When Graham spoke of God creating the heavens, Zamperini experienced a new set of flashbacks: floating in the vast Pacific under the beautiful star-filled sky. The sky had testified to God's goodness, and Zamperini, hovering near death in a rubber raft, had responded.

When Graham spoke of God's miracles and intangible blessings, Zamperini remembered the crash of his bomber, when he was dragged underwater in the airplane fuselage, wrapped in wires. He passed out and breathed in ocean water, then for some reason, awoke to find the wires that had trapped him underwater inexplicably gone. He made it to the surface and caught hold of a raft floating nearby. Had that been God's doing?

He recalled a Japanese bomber strafing their raft, missing him and his two companions even while riddling the raft with bullet holes. Had that been God?

Zamperini found himself entranced by Graham's words. But then, when Graham began to urge a response of faith, Zamperini reacted angrily. He jumped to his feet, pushed past people in his row of seats, and made for the exit. He felt enraged, trapped, on the edge of explosion. Just as he reached the aisle, another memory came. One day when he was lying exhausted, desiccated, and hopeless after six days in the tropical sun without water, he had made a promise to God. *If you will save me, I will serve you forever.* As though in response, the skies opened and dumped torrents of warm, sweet rain.

He had promised God, and God had rescued him. But he had never fulfilled his pledge.

Zamperini suddenly turned in the other direction. Rather than charging out of the tent, he went to the front of the assembly, to the foot of the stage where Graham was offering prayer and counsel. That night, Zamperini prayed to God to forgive him, to cleanse his heart and make him a new man. He went home and poured all his alcohol down the drain. His nightmares disappeared. The rest of his life, he dedicated to forgiveness. He even traveled to Japan to visit some of his prison guards, now imprisoned themselves, to tell them that he forgave him. (The Bird, sadly, refused to see him.)

* *

Most probably you *will* reach the end of the rope sometime in your life. When you get dumped by the person you love. When your carefully planned career meets a disastrous roadblock. When repeated rejection convinces you that you are utterly without talent. When you realize that you are really addicted, and can't get free.

David and Zamperini followed parallel tracks. They experienced enormous success, then enormous suffering, then deep bitterness and despair. Just when they were utterly undone, they were able to turn to God and find hope.

Did David's Son, Jesus, ever face such total loss? Of course he did. He was pushed to the brink by hostile and envious religious leaders, put on trial, tortured, executed—all totally alone, with his best friends and followers nowhere to be seen.

Unlike David, he never lied, never pretended to be something other than what he was, never hurt or damaged others in order to escape punishment.

Like David, he did find strength in God. "Father, into your hands I commit my spirit."

Sometimes when we talk about facing failure, we really mean facing adversity. We mean facing setbacks. We mean "when the going gets tough, the tough get going."

But failure can be far more complete, and far more devastating. Sometimes you lose everything that matters to you—loved ones, friends, future. Sometimes you lose your sense of who you are.

Then comes the ultimate test. Can you find strength in God? Can you rediscover hope? Can you remember what you promised God?

You may need your equivalent of David's ephod, an instrument that enables you to direct questions to God and receive direction.

What does that look like for you? Retreat? A day—or days—away from the stresses of everyday life, to make yourself available to hear God in the space of unplanned time? To find your direction in company with him?

Some people go into the wilderness (or to a retreat center), but others stay at home to take a time of worship and fasting. They devote blocks of time to praying the psalms, David's prayers.

Some find a spiritual director, a trained companion for the road of life, a guide for the spiritual journey. They especially rely on this person during times of stress or great difficulty.

Some go on pilgrimages, which have a long tradition of helping seekers find new light for their path. The most famous pilgrimage is the Camino de Santiago, which begins in France and winds its way (on foot) for hundreds of miles through northern Spain. On this and other routes, pilgrims encounter others who are seeking direction.

This is just a sampling of many devices that people use to find strength in God when they face great loss.

No matter how successful, you are not immune to failure. If and when it comes, it may seem like the end of your life. It's not. You can find strength in God. You can structure your life in small ways or large to ask God questions and listen for his direction. David did. Louis Zamperini did. Jesus did.

QUESTION FOR MEDITATION

What's the worst you can imagine? How would you respond?

6. ON TOP OF THE WORLD

PART 1

Disaster is always a possibility on the road to success, but so is its opposite. Sometimes you go through a streak of life when everything turns out in your favor. Success just rolls your way. You'd like to take credit for it, but you know you can't.

For myself, I think of my role in creating *The Student Bible*, by far the most successful project I've ever been involved in. It's a Bible with notes that has sold almost seven million copies. I'm proud that I was part of it, but I am well aware that I was undeservedly blessed—what you might call lucky.*

In the first place, it wasn't my idea. My friend and colleague Philip Yancey had the vision, and he pushed hard to make it happen. He presented it to a publisher, Zondervan, and got them to fund its development. The idea—which nowadays seems quite obvious but at the time was novel—was to add notes to the Bible that would help inexperienced Bible readers to understand it. It wasn't a new idea to have a Bible with explanatory notes, but up to then, those notes had been in tiny print at the bottom of the page, and they were usually dense explanations of

---

* I use the word "lucky" though well aware that it can be misinterpreted. I mean simply to say, I don't know why this happened to me and not somebody else. It wasn't because of my virtues. I see lots of good people who don't get lucky, and I see plenty of bad people who do. Of course, as a Christian, I know that underneath everything that happens is God, but I often can't explain why things happen as they do. "Lucky" is a way of retaining the mystery of God's will.

theological or historical points. Philip wanted to add something more like CliffsNotes: easier to understand than the original. He was going to do it all himself, reading scholarly commentaries on all the books of the Bible and translating their insights into a journalistic style that would be interesting, relevant, and understandable. He would write for those, young or old, who wanted to read the Bible but found it overwhelming and difficult. The notes in *The Student Bible* were intended to help them over the hump, orienting and explaining and encouraging.

Philip and I had talked about this, but I wasn't involved. I had a full-time job in Africa. At any rate, I wasn't that enthused. The project was Philip's dream, not mine.

Philip went to work and discovered, as does everybody who tries to survey the entire Bible, that it is a very big book. Getting through the New Testament took him so long that he knew he needed help with the Old if he wasn't going to collect Social Security before he finished. That was when he invited me to work with him, strictly on a contract basis.

By then, I was coming home from Kenya, and I needed a job. The Bible would tide me over until I figured out the next step. Philip explained to me that he had an editorial plan very well mapped out. I wasn't asked to be creative, just to follow the plan.

I took the job gladly. I needed the money, and I thought it would do me good to study the Old Testament in more depth. I began work on Jeremiah, a very long and somewhat daunting book. Before I had gone too far, however, Philip and I got distressing news.

Our publisher had produced Philip's work-to-date as a paperback New Testament. They printed 50,000 copies of *Insight* with his notes. *Insight* was meant to be an appetizer. People would read it and want more; they would seek out the whole Bible when it came out sometime later.

The distressing news was that *Insight* didn't sell. It was not a mere disappointment. It was a complete flop. Zondervan shipped out 50,000 copies, and nearly all of them came back. Hardly anybody wanted one.

Our friends at Zondervan suddenly became rather cold. They stopped picking up the lunch check. We couldn't get a meeting with their key personnel. Years later, some of the executives admitted to us that they came very close to pulling the plug on the whole project.

Philip and I couldn't really blame them. We realized we had a problem and that we were the only people who could fix it, assuming that it was fixable. We began doing research. We met with many people who might have insight into how inexperienced readers approached the Bible. We did focus groups. We read anything we thought might be helpful. Some of what we learned was really different from what we had expected. For example, we had thought that using photographs as illustrations would make the Bible seem more relevant. We learned, instead, that inexperienced Bible readers treasure the Bible as a holy book, and photos seemed too casual to them.

Philip and I talked and talked about what we were learning and tried out different ideas of how we might make our Bible better. It took us the better part of a year, but we came up with a new approach. The goal was the same, but we changed the editorial framework.

This required reworking all that Philip had already completed, plus writing all the Old Testament notes. It took years. With the help of a great young graphic designer, Nate Young, we finally brought out the first edition. I remember talking to Philip when the Bible was finally ready to appear in print. "It probably won't make any difference," I said with resignation, "but at least we can truthfully say we did our best."

Zondervan, our publisher, had low expectations. We wished they would promote our Bible more, but we couldn't really blame them for going slow. Indeed, initial sales were modest—not disastrous, but modest.

Most books have their largest sale in the first few months, and then taper off. We expected that result with *The Student Bible*, and we were surprised when it didn't happen. Sales remained modest, but they didn't go down, either. Six months to a year later, sales actually increased. They increased steadily to a much higher level, and then they held steady at that, year after year. The realization slowly came over us: we had a success on our hands. A big success. It wasn't just reflected in the numbers, which I got in a long printout every three months. It was also that I began to see people carrying *The Student Bible* and to hear from people who appreciated it.

I write this 35 years after *The Student Bible* came out. During those years, I've watched in wonder as the project I took on as "just a job" has carved out a place in the world.

For 35 years, I've felt undeservedly blessed. Lucky! Remember, it wasn't my dream. I never expected much to come of it. I can't claim much credit. (It's a bit weird anyway to take credit for the Bible.) I'm incredibly grateful, however, for the chance to be part of it. I'm grateful too for Philip's great generosity in writing me into the contract so I got a small royalty once we paid Zondervan back for their initial advance. That made it possible for me to try writing projects I wouldn't otherwise have been able to afford.

You can be lucky in love, lucky at work, lucky at sports, lucky at anything that matters to you. I'm lucky to be born an American, lucky to have wonderful parents. The response is obvious: be thankful. And don't go thinking that you are too special, that you did it yourself.

* *

My experience with *The Student Bible* is nothing compared to David's. He went on a winning streak that lasted ten years. Everything went right for him.

It didn't look like that at first. Picture him, standing in Ziklag with his band of men. Only days before, they were ready to kill him. Now, they rejoice: they have rescued their wives and children. They're not out of trouble, however. The town they stand in has been burned to the ground. They can provide their families no shelter from the elements, no spare clothes, no stockpiled grain. Besides, they have no future. Israel doesn't want them—and may want them less, if word gets out that they marched with the Philistine army. Philistines don't want them either—they sent them back from the battle. Six hundred men cannot survive as a law unto themselves in this violent Palestinian environment.

For three days, they squat in the ashes, unsure what to do. Then a man staggers into town, his clothes torn and his hair clotted with dirt. He finds his way to David and bows low. The Israelite army has been routed, he reports, and Saul and Jonathan are dead.

The man claims to be an eyewitness. After the battle, probably as he searched the corpses to see if he could scavenge anything valuable, he happened upon Saul, half-dead. Saul begged the man to finish him off, he says. He did what Saul requested: he killed him. Taking Saul's crown and his armband, he brought them to David.

The man surely expects that David will reward him for bringing this news. Surely David will be ecstatic! His nemesis is dead! The man must be surprised when David rips the expensive fabric of his shirt all down the front and sets up a cry of distress. David's men watch their leader, then imitate him. They all begin to mourn for Saul, wailing like coyotes. They sing laments for Saul and Jonathan and the nation of Israel and for all the people of Israel, their near relations. They are not putting on a show. They undoubtedly feel some gladness that Saul, their tormentor, is gone, but they fix their attention on Israel's loss. Their king and his heir are killed and the army routed. The nation is decapitated, and from this day forward, foreigners rule. They know these foreigners; they are violent and cruel.

All day long, they mourn. After the sun sets, they break their fast by slaughtering sheep from the herd and roasting them on a fire. David calls the man who brought the news. "Where are you from?" he asks him.

"I am the son of an Amalekite immigrant," he says.

"Why weren't you afraid to kill God's anointed king?" David asks. He stares at the Amalekite, who says nothing.

David calls to one of his aides. "Come here," he says. "Stab him."

Obedience comes instinctively to David's men, and so does violence. With one thrust, David's aide kills the Amalekite. David stands over the body and announces for all to hear, "You deserved to die. You said yourself, 'I finished off God's anointed king.'"

David then picks up his lyre, which he has been playing mournfully all day, and introduces a song he has just written.

> Daughters of Israel,
> weep for Saul,
> who clothed you in scarlet and finery,
> who adorned your garments with ornaments of gold.

> How the mighty have fallen in battle!
> Jonathan lies slain on your heights.
> I grieve for you, Jonathan my brother;
> you were very dear to me.
> Your love for me was wonderful,
> more wonderful than that of women.

> How the mighty have fallen!
> The weapons of war have perished! (2 Samuel 1:24–27)

With the song, he honors both the man who was his best and only friend, and the man's father who tried to kill David. David chooses to recall the best of Saul, and he sings of his deep love for Jonathan. It is a lament that will be sung for generations to come.

Though David makes no mention of God, he has not forgotten him. The next morning, he calls for the ephod and asks God whether he should go settle in one of the Judean towns. If so, which one? He is unsure where he will be welcome, if anywhere. The answer comes: go to Hebron.

Hebron is in the hill country, not too many miles from Ziklag. What with children and sheep, the journey takes days. But Hebron welcomes them. Absorbing 600 families cannot be easy, but there are big benefits for Hebron. David's militia brings considerable protection to the town. Remember, the Philistine army has just defeated Israel's and is very much on the loose.

Word gets around to the other Judean towns and villages. They put together a delegation that comes to Hebron for an audience with David. They want him to be their king. On the spot, they pour oil on his head and anoint him. The Bible does not report David's emotions, but how can he be anything less than overwhelmed? A short time before, he was a man without a country, pursued by his own bloodthirsty king. Now he is settled into his home territory, and—without even a fight—he has been anointed king. It is an extraordinary reversal, and he did nothing to arrange it—just survive.

* *

Favor piles on top of favor. A lengthy civil war ensues between David's troops and Saul's supporters, but in the end, the elders of the northern tribes come to David and pledge their loyalty. They have little choice, really. They need a king to rally the fighters against the Philistines, and the last qualified heir to Saul is dead. It does not hurt that David has done nothing to hurt Saul or his heirs. He mourned their loss, showing sympathy for the feelings of the people of the north.

Without lifting a finger, David becomes king of all Israel.

As king, he is very active indeed. He conquers Jerusalem and makes it his capital. Considered impregnable, the mountain fortress falls to David and his men. The new capital has a unifying effect on Israel. Centrally located, it does not lie in the territory of any tribe but gathers them all.

David is a great commander, and in a series of battles, he manages to drive out the Philistine occupiers. Peace comes to Israel—a very scarce and precious commodity.

At the same time, David does what all kings do: he accumulates wives and concubines and produces children. He came to Hebron with two wives; in Jerusalem, he acquires a royal harem and sires many children.

Finally, he makes a point of seeking out Saul's last remaining grandson, Jonathan's son, Mephibosheth. He is crippled in both legs due to a childhood accident; as such, he can never be king. Nonetheless, he has lived in hiding since his father died, because he fears David.

Now, David summons him to Jerusalem —for what else, Mephibosheth thinks, than further retribution? David intends not clan vengeance, however, but love. He promised Jonathan that their loyalty would extend into generations to come. (1 Samuel 20:42) Now, he lives up to that promise. To show kindness to Jonathan's son, David gives him his grandfather's land and assigns his grandfather's steward to farm it for him. Mephibosheth will live and eat at the palace, like family.

David's treatment of Mephibosheth is a powerful and public statement of his values. His reign will remember friends—even friends from the wrong tribe. The weak and disabled will be included. He will reach out across barriers, in love, to bring all Israelites together.

Second Samuel 5 summarizes: "David grew greater and greater, and the Lord of Hosts was with him." (2 Samuel 5:10, Alter) A few lines later it adds, "David knew that the Lord had set him up unshaken as king over Israel." (5:12)

David has gone from a sheep-herding boy to tormented exile to king of Israel. He knows his transformation is due to something deeper than his leadership expertise. He knows that God had set him up unshaken; he owes everything to God.

Some of David's songs allude to his sense of astonished gratefulness:

> He reached down from on high and took hold of me;
>> he drew me out of deep waters.
> He rescued me from my powerful enemy,
>> from my foes, who were too strong for me...
> He brought me out into a spacious place;
>> he rescued me because he delighted in me. (Psalm 18:16–19)

If the Lord had not been on our side —
    let Israel say—
if the Lord had not been on our side
    when people attacked us,
they would have swallowed us alive…

Praise be to the Lord,
    who has not let us be torn by their teeth.
We have escaped like a bird
    from the fowler's snare;
the snare has been broken,
    and we have escaped. (Psalm 124:1–3, 5–6)

* *

When people experience great success, it usually doesn't take long for them to forget that luck had anything to do with it. Their friends and family congratulate them, so they congratulate themselves. Other people fawn on them, so they fawn on themselves. They attribute their success entirely to talent and hard work.

David was different. He was deeply amazed and consistently gave credit to God. How do I know? Read the psalms. Not once does David tell God what a great man he is. (He does tell God that he has faithfully followed God's commandments.) No, he tells God what a great God he is. He doesn't brag about himself or his army or his nation. He brags about God. He praises God.

If you are already successful, you should be like David, humbly thanking God. If you are not yet successful, you need to prepare for success by learning thankfulness and praise for whatever you have been given so far. Make thanksgiving a habit, and it will come naturally the rest of your life. Neglect it, and you won't remember it when your time in the spotlight comes.

David knew that behind every streak of luck is a loving God. David gives God the credit in his psalms. (He also complains and moans to God about everything that goes wrong.) There is no evidence that David saw himself as the hero of his story. God is the hero of David's story.

For Jesus, David's Son, it's the same. He sees God at work everywhere, and he wants to teach his followers to see the world in the same way. He does amazing healings, and preaches wonderful sermons, and attracts huge and astonished crowds, but he doesn't focus attention on himself at all. When he heals people, he actually urges them to tell nobody about it! He turns attention to God and encourages faith. That is the right way to respond, when things go your way.

QUESTION FOR MEDITATION

When things go your way, is it your instinct to be grateful?
Or to take all the credit you can get?

2 Samuel 6, 7

7. ON TOP OF THE WORLD
PART 2

My wedding day was the happiest day of my life. Driving to the church with my friend Fred, I began to cry for pure joy. I could not stop; I could not get the breath to explain to Fred what was happening to me. Generally speaking, I never cry, and certainly not from joy. Fred did not press me to explain; he merely reached out and offered me a clean handkerchief.

Popie and I had known each other for years, mainly as long-distance friends. I lived in Chicago; she lived in Palo Alto, and we saw each other only a few times a year, usually when I had work that took me to the West Coast. We corresponded occasionally. There was mutual admiration, but nothing romantic.

Then I fell in love, suddenly and explosively. For a very long time—it seemed like eternity, although it was less than two years—Popie was disinterested in romance with me. She preferred to be just friends. I found it terribly painful. Why couldn't I forget her? I tried, but I only suffered.

Then one day, without any advance warning, she told me that she had changed her mind. The sun came out, dispersing the darkness. Birds learned to sing. My life changed. Within a year, I was driving to my wedding, crying for joy.

Our ceremony was a worship service full of God. We were so full of gratefulness that thanking God was the most natural thing we could imagine. We sang, we prayed. Sitting on top of the world, we felt very close to heaven.

* *

David, suddenly on top of the world, wants God's ark—his earthly throne, the symbol of his presence—to be near.

For so many years as a fugitive, David was kept far from the tabernacle where the ark resided. Sleeping in the bush, always on the alert for betrayal, he could not go the tabernacle to make sacrifices, to celebrate festivals, and to acclaim God's presence. He could not join the people of God in their holy feasts, to worship God as he wanted.

Can you imagine his longing? Probably not, if you're an American. But those in places where the church is banned can feel what David felt.

Now, he is king of Israel, secure in his new capital and palace, living with his wives and children. He wants God to be part of it. He wants his life to be lived close to the place of worship. In his mind, this means moving the ark to new quarters—to Jerusalem.

The whole of Israel should be involved in the relocation, he believes. No doubt this is partly a political gesture: David has gone to great lengths to unify Israel after a long civil war. Locating the ark in Jerusalem, the new capital, will bring all the tribes together. As the story develops, however, we see that for David, moving the ark is very personal.

* *

One morning before dawn, a huge throng gathers in front of David's palace. Thirty thousand men have come to accompany the ark to Jerusalem. They crowd together in the street, stamping their feet, greeting old friends. The sound is like the dull rumble of the sea. Then David emerges. When they see him, they cheer. He leads the jostling procession through the streets and out the gate. A long stream of men follows David on the road to Baalah, a little hilltop town ten miles west. That is where the ark landed after multiple moves during the long unsettled pre-David era.

By mid-morning, the procession has gathered around a private home where the ark is stored. The homeowner's sons have the privilege of driving a new-made oxcart carrying the ark to Jerusalem. Apparently, it does not occur to anyone to consult the biblical manual, which is quite explicit about how to move the ark. It is a big box fitted with rings on both sides. The rings are for poles, and the poles are meant to assist Levites, the hereditary keepers of the tabernacle, when they need to move the ark. According to divine regulation, that is the only way to move the ark—by Levite. Furthermore, no one is to touch the ark. It is too holy to be profaned by any human hand. (Exodus 25:10–16, Numbers 4:15)

No one is thinking about such matters. They are too busy celebrating. David is in the lead with his lyre. Others bash rhythm instruments, and every man in the procession sings lustily in praise to God. I imagine a sound like you hear at soccer games: a deep-toned, almost tuneless mass song of celebration. What joy! Decades of fear and oppression and division are being sloughed off. They have a new king and a new capital. God is in it all; God gave it all. So they sing and forget their old worries. They are on top of the world, near to heaven.

Then, suddenly, the procession lurches to a stop. Ripples of alarm spread through the crowd. Only a few people saw what happened, but word spreads. The brace of oxen pulling the cart slipped on a steep place in the road, and the cart tilted sideways. Fearing that the ark would fall out, one of the cart drivers put out a hand to hold it steady—and fell to the ground. By the time David reaches him, he is stone dead.

David walks angrily away from the body. He has no doubt who is responsible. In the midst of celebration, without warning, God lashed out and took a young man's life.

David has been so sure of himself in bringing the ark to Jerusalem, thinking that he does something pleasing to God—believing, in fact, that he does God a favor. And how does God respond? Without a word of warning, he kills.

Can David live with such a God? Does he want to be near such an explosive God? Do good intentions count for nothing? For surely the driver meant no harm in reaching out to steady the ark.

They are passing by a big farm. Impetuously, David orders the ark removed from the cart. Men are slow to obey; they saw what happened.

Gingerly, using the prescribed poles, they lift the ark and carry it into the barn. There they leave it. Silently, sullenly, the procession straggles the remaining miles back to Jerusalem.

* *

His experience with the ark upsets David deeply. In his songs, he has said a hundred times that God is powerful, but he didn't expect to see a man struck dead for touching a holy object. Why would God respond so violently to a simple mistake? It seems massively unfair to David.

For three months, David nurses his hurt feelings toward God. Let the ark sit in a barn! See if he cares! Then he hears surprising reports. Evidently the farm owner is delighted to have the ark on his property. Everything seems to go extra well for him now. Crops flourish; the fields are heavy with grain. Sheep and goats multiply. Healthy babies are born. Sick family members begin to eat heartily and put on weight.

This news makes David rethink his grudge against God. God's ark may be a source of danger, but it is also obviously a source of blessing.

He has to admit he treated the ark lightly, acting like God was just a big, friendly family dog. Now he begins learning a deeper lesson. Thankfulness needs to be combined with proper humility. God is God. He not only deserves our thanks, he demands our respect. Total respect.

David may never understand why God demands that the ark be treated with such absolute precision. However, the instructions are clear enough for anybody to follow, if they care to pay attention. The responsibility for the offense doesn't ultimately lie with the cart driver, who paid with his life. It lies with David. He was the person in charge.

David owes God an apology. A big apology.

So, David organizes Israelites far and wide to return to the farm and escort the ark into Jerusalem. This time, they do it according to regulations. David adds a layer of worship to the procession, donning a priest's costume and sacrificing a bull to God at the very beginning of the march. Most of all, David throws himself into the dance as he never has, whirling and jigging, a picture of joy. He gets caught up into it. The whole crowd takes his cue, shouting and blowing horns as they dance their way into the city. They carry the ark to a tent David has erected, and there David himself offers sacrifices to God, pronouncing blessings on the people in God's name, and distributing food for people to take home for a feast. It is a great and unforgettable day in Jerusalem. At last, the ark has come.

When the celebration is over, David returns to his home. His wife Michal comes to the door to greet him. She is spoiling for a fight.

Michal has suffered a great deal in her life. She married David out of love, but when David ran for his life—and she saved his skin—her father gave her to another man. Imagine what that was like! David demanded her back when the civil war ended, but no longer as his sole wife. She is now one of many.

She is a proud woman, a king's daughter who has been treated like disposable property. Watching from a window while David dances into town, she scorns him for his lack of dignity. She is from royalty; he is acting like trailer trash. As he comes back home, she cannot hold her tongue.

"How the king of Israel has distinguished himself today, going around half-naked in full view of the slave girls of his servants as any vulgar fellow would!"

David is tired. He got up early and danced for hours. It has been a great day, and now his own wife gives him grief for his love of God. Stressful situations bring out the worst and the best in people. In David, Michal's disgust provokes an angry but magnificent response:

"It was before the LORD, who chose me rather than your father or anyone from his house when he appointed me ruler over the LORD's people Israel—I will celebrate before the LORD. I will become even more undignified than this, and I will be humiliated in my own eyes. But by these slave girls you spoke of, I will be held in honor." (2 Samuel 6:21–22)

David is on top of the world, and no one will deprive him of God. If it is undignified to worship extravagantly, he will be undignified. He cares only for God's reputation, not his own.

There is a lesson here. In our moments of greatest success, we will encounter those who want us to play it cool, who prefer that we not speak too sincerely of God, who find it amusing that God is given credit even though he is nowhere to be seen. David is a model of how to respond: claim it. When you are on top of the world, God belongs there with you.

* *

As David contemplates the ark's place in Jerusalem, he begins to feel that he has—for all his whirling and dancing—still failed to give God the honor he deserves. David has built himself a palace. God still lives in a tent. He would like to build God a palace.

It's a universal urge. All religions build shrines. The glory of those shrines (or churches, tabernacles, temples, mosques) reflects the glory of their Higher Power. People don't want to worship just anywhere; they want a permanent place and a beautiful place.

David puts it to a prophet, Nathan, who encourages him to go ahead. That night, however, God appears to Nathan and gives him a different memorandum. The basic message for David is blunt to the edge of rudeness: Thanks, but no thanks. Who told you that you should provide a home for me?

Chronicles adds that God tells David he is too bloodstained for such an honor. (1 Chronicles 22:8) That must come as a shock. David takes pride in his warrior prowess; it is his main claim to fame in Israel. "Saul has killed his thousands, and David his tens of thousands." God has a different view; he is repulsed by the bloodshed. (And so will be Jesus, David's son, God's Son, a king who will never kill.)

For David, who is (again) feeling very generous toward God, it is a strong rebuff. God, who placed David on top of the world, is not interested in being his charity case. When he wants a new place to live, he will get one for himself.

But that is not the end of the message. God also wants to remind David how intimately and thoroughly he has been involved in David's success, every step of the way. "I took you from the pasture, from tending the flock, and appointed you ruler over my people Israel. I have been with you wherever you have gone." (2 Samuel 7:8, 9) That includes the endless hours watching sheep, and the long, anxious nights hiding out from Saul in the wilderness. It includes even his lost months as a Philistine mercenary. God was there all along.

God announces that he intends to make his permanent residence in David's family: David's dynasty will be God's true "house." Israel will be free from fear and unoppressed by enemies. One of David's sons— not David—will construct a building to house the ark and will adopt an intimate, father-son relationship with God himself.

Psalm 132 tells the story:

> The Lord swore an oath to David,
>   a sure oath he will not revoke:
> "One of your own descendants
>   I will place on your throne.
> If your sons keep my covenant

and the statutes I teach them,
then their sons will sit
on your throne for ever and ever." (Psalm 132:11–12)

To this point, Nathan has been David's go-between, taking messages to God and receiving messages from God. Now, shaken, David quietly walks to the tent where the ark is kept. He needs to talk to God directly.

He might have been offended that God dressed him down. Most monarchs dislike being put in their place. But David's words say nothing about that. They are full of humility and awe. "Who am I, Lord God, that you have brought me this far? ...Lord God, there is none like you and there is no god beside you." (2 Samuel 7:18, 22)

This is the way to be on top of the world: recognizing that you are there only because God has taken you there.

* *

A moment came in Jesus' work when his kingdom began to be visible to those who had eyes to see it. He had preached and done miracles to general astonishment. He had gathered disciples and sent them out on his mission. He had glimpsed the beginnings of resistance to his work, which only revealed how petty the opposition was. Jesus came out with these amazing words:

> "I praise you, Father, Lord of heaven and earth, because
> you have hidden these things from the wise and learned,
> and revealed them to little children. Yes, Father, for this
> is what you were pleased to do."
>
> "All things have been committed to me by my Father.
> No one knows the Son except the Father, and no one
> knows the Father except the Son and those to whom
> the Son chooses to reveal him."
>
> "Come to me, all you who are weary and burdened,
> and I will give you rest. Take my yoke upon you and
> learn from me, for I am gentle and humble in heart, and
> you will find rest for your souls. For my yoke is easy and
> my burden is light." (Matthew 11:25–30)

The promises made to David were coming true in Jesus, David's Son. Jesus was an indestructible house for God.

Jesus explained it to a woman he met at a well. She tried to dodge his questions by raising a theological argument about the true Temple. Was it Jesus' Jewish one in Jerusalem, or her tribe's on Mt. Gerizim? Jesus would have none of that argument. He told the woman, "God is Spirit, and his worshipers must worship in the Spirit and in truth." (John 4:24)

Jesus was the Son of David building God's Temple—a building made up of Spirit-filled lives. He was completing David's story. Like David at his best, he was humbly amazed at what God had done for him. Like David at his best, his triumph never belonged to him alone; it was for God and God's people. This is success at its best.

* *

Thankfulness with humility does not come easily to successful people. Typically, they think they deserve everything they got; that their genius, hard work, passion, creativity, and (usually) good looks got them to the top of the mountain. They think this even if they inherited it all from Daddy!

Jesus told his disciples that it's easier to push a camel through the eye of a needle than to push a rich person into the kingdom of God. The reason is humility, or lack of it. It comes hard to rich people. It comes hard to successful people.

You only counteract this through persistent, daily practice.

That starts with worship, in which we glorify God, not ourselves. We count our blessings: in daily prayer, in a journal, in our weekly small group, in Sunday worship, actively thanking God for each gift, and acknowledging it came from him.

We practice crediting God when we describe events of our day or week. "I'm thankful to God for keeping me safe; I had some close calls." "I passed my exam; I was so worried but I prayed to God for help." "What a beautiful day! Isn't God good!"

It can certainly be thoughtless and annoying to wrap every event in God-talk, but there are ways to do this that are natural and don't draw undue attention to themselves. It's an art form. That's why we need practice.

I just saw a friend, an artist, whom I've watched struggle to make a name for herself over many years. She feels a very strong sense of God's calling her to paint, but painting is a difficult taskmaster. She can be a terrible critic of herself. And meanwhile, there are so many artists, it's hard to even get people to look at what she's done, let alone buy it. She, like most artists, can feel very alone and unappreciated.

Just now, after years of persisting, my friend is seeing a breakthrough. Suddenly, several galleries want to show her work and she's accepted to prestigious shows. At our bi-monthly Bible study, she shared her joy. She wanted to say what a gift it is: not something she deserves, but God's graciousness made visible. She is doing what she believes God called her to do—painting—and she keeps on doing it, regardless of the weather. Suddenly, the sun has come out.

My friend cited this passage from the Message Bible translation: "Be content with who you are, and don't put on airs. God's strong hand is on you; he'll promote you at the right time. Live carefree before God; he is most careful with you." (1 Peter 5:6, 7)

Jesus models this when he speaks of the cluelessness of people he has preached to. "I praise you, Father, Lord of heaven and earth, because you have hidden these things from the wise and learned, and revealed them to little children. Yes, Father, for this is what you were pleased to do." Those words brim over with happy trust in God—even though, clearly, the "wise and learned" aren't getting the message.

And then Jesus makes this beautiful offer: "Come to me, all you who are weary and burdened, and I will give you rest. Take my yoke upon you and learn from me, for I am gentle and humble in heart, and you will find rest for your souls. For my yoke is easy and my burden is light." (Matthew 11:25–26, 28–30)

David, on top of the world, missed the target initially. He tried to put himself in the role of God's benefactor. Thankfully, God corrected him and gave him a second chance. He will do that with you, too.

QUESTION FOR MEDITATION

When you are on top of the world, what might keep you from humility?

8. GOVERNMENT BY WORDS

America has been a nation for more than 200 years, and during that time, thousands of laws have been passed. They were written by members of Congress, passed by the House of Representatives and the Senate, and signed by the President. Then the President and his administration applied the laws to the people of the United States, often creating regulations to spell out the practicalities.

This is largely what we mean by "government." It's about writing, passing, and applying the law.

However, the United States is also governed by a second set of words—words that have no legal standing. Three documents stand out. The first and most foundational is the Declaration of Independence, written largely by Thomas Jefferson. Its most important words are these:

> *We hold these truths to be self-evident, that all men are created equal, that they are endowed by their Creator with certain unalienable Rights, that among these are Life, Liberty and the pursuit of Happiness. — That to secure these rights, Governments are instituted among Men, deriving their just powers from the consent of the governed.*

Jefferson wrote these words while holding slaves as property. He (and others who signed the Declaration) were inconsistent, to put it the gentlest way. Nevertheless, the Declaration of Independence became the conscience of the nation, calling Americans to a more just and equal society. It calls us still.

A second document, the Gettysburg Address, was merely a speech, written to mark a significant occasion. In it, President Abraham Lincoln referred to the Declaration of Independence as the founding ideal of America, and he called a nation battered by civil war to rededicate itself to becoming a nation of freedom, "of the people, by the people, for the people."

A third document, Martin Luther King's "I have a dream" speech, did not even arise within government. King was a pastor, preaching to a congregation that was as wide as America. He, too, spoke of the Declaration of Independence and applied it to a nation divided by race. "I have a dream that my four little children will one day live in a nation where they will not be judged by the color of their skin but by the content of their character."

What makes America great? What holds it together through stressful times? These deep, enduring words, as much as anything.

* *

David was unquestionably a skillful leader, but what made him a great king was poetry. Most of his poems come down to us in the Book of Psalms, a collection that functioned something like a hymnbook in Israel. That means people learned them, memorized them, used them for their own prayers, and spoke them aloud in temple and synagogue. Half of the Psalms are attributed to David, often in just two words: "Of David."

What makes poetry great? I don't think anybody can define that, but you know it when you hear it. David's poems are great. They are great literature, but they are more than that. They are songs that formed the very heart of Israel. To this very day, 3,000 years later, this poetry is memorized by children and sung by believers. To this day, it stirs hearts and brings tears to people's eyes.

David was a warrior who defeated the Philistines and provided national security. His military prowess proved to be a short-term legacy, however. Israel was never very good at war. The nation lost as many wars as it won and was ultimately decimated by foreign powers. Where ancient Israel excelled was in passionate relationship to God. Their faith we remember and learn from to this day. We learn it first and foremost through the Psalms.

The Russian author Alexander Solzhenitsyn wrote, "For a country to have a great writer ... is like having a second government." Even while David was in hiding, fearing for his life, his poems were writing a new way of life for his people. In making poetry, David was building a great nation.

* *

When Winston Churchill became Prime Minister of Great Britain on May 10, 1940, Nazi Germany seemed likely to subdue all of Europe, including Britain, through savage military might. Churchill knew his country was outgunned in terms of airplanes, tanks, and well-trained soldiers. He fought the war with different weapons: words.

> I would say to the House as I said to those who have joined this government: I have nothing to offer but blood, toil, tears and sweat. We have before us an ordeal of the most grievous kind. We have before us many, many long months of struggle and of suffering.
>
> You ask, what is our policy? I will say: It is to wage war, by sea, land and air, with all our might and with all the strength that God can give us; to wage war against a monstrous tyranny, never surpassed in the dark and lamentable catalogue of human crime. That is our policy. You ask, what is our aim? I can answer in one word: Victory. Victory at all costs—Victory in spite of all terror—Victory, however long and hard the road may be, for without victory there is no survival.

As the Battle of Britain began and the threat of invasion became an immediate and genuine fear, Churchill's defiant words continued:

> ... we shall fight in France, we shall fight on the seas and oceans, we shall fight with growing confidence and growing strength in the air, we shall defend our island, whatever the cost may be, we shall fight on the beaches, we shall fight on the landing grounds, we shall fight in the fields and in the streets, we shall fight in the hills; we shall never surrender.

Churchill's speeches created hope out of thin air. He faced grim realities, mustering courage to overcome them. He led the fight against Germany, not by commandeering a tank or piloting a plane or shooting a gun. He did it all with words.

* *

The earliest passage in the Bible that is indisputably poetry is Exodus 15:1–18, the Song of Moses and Miriam. The first words give it away: "I will sing." You sing in poetry. Moses and Miriam sang a rollicking praise song to God, who rescued his people from the Egyptians.

Moses is also the author of a song in Deuteronomy 32. That poem tells the history of a wonderful God who chooses Israel as his people, and a faithless people who constantly go astray.

These themes from Moses—praise and triumph, a gracious God and a faithless people—get repeated many times in the Bible, particularly in the poetry of the prophets. Most of what the prophets say has to do with justice—the justice Israel owes the poor, and (even more) the justice Israel owes God. Your neighbor deserves more! the prophets say. Your God deserves much more!

David's psalms, however, speak in an utterly different voice. In them you hear the unmistakable tone of an individual speaking personally to God. David's prayers are passionate and intimate. He is frustrated by circumstances. He fears his enemies. He pleads for mercy and basks in God's love. There is darkness and light, cheer and gloom, guilt and forgiveness, praise and pleas for help. This is why David's psalms have captured the hearts of believers for thousands of years: each one of us lives with hopes and fears; each one of us can adopt these poems as our own.

Praying the psalms, a person affirms that *life is difficult.* Yes, there is joy and exultation in God and all he has done. But there is also much complaining, questioning, worrying. Each person praying the psalms becomes like Jacob, wrestling with God and demanding that God bless him. This personal wrestling stands opposed to many forms of religion that are dominated by law and doctrine. That kind of religion puts many demands on people; it makes them feel small. If you talk to people who have left their faith in rebellion or despair, very often, their fundamental complaint boils down to this: there was no room for me.

In the Psalms, there is always plenty of room for me.

David's legacy is this personal, intimate engagement with God. The individual may (and must) speak with complete honesty. We bring all of ourselves to God, even the parts we don't like.

* *

In David's prayers, certain themes come through again and again:

Enemies. The great biblical scholar Derek Kidner noted two fundamental realities that appear in virtually all the Psalms: the presence of God, and the presence of enemies. Time and again, David presents these enemies to God, asking for protection and vindication.

> Lord, how many are my foes!
>   How many rise up against me!
> Many are saying of me,
>   "God will not deliver him."
> ~Psalm 3:1, 2

Security. David is sometimes frantic with worry, but he repeatedly returns to the comfort and security of resting in God. He expresses this with great, convincing eloquence:

> Even though I walk
>   through the darkest valley,
> I will fear no evil,
>   for you are with me;
> your rod and your staff,
>   they comfort me.
> ~Psalm 23:4

Seeking help. David engages a God who sees his troubles, who can hear his plea.

> But you, Sovereign Lord,
>   help me for your name's sake;

> out of the goodness of your love, deliver me.
> For I am poor and needy,
>   and my heart is wounded within me.
> ~Psalm 109:21–22

Asking mercy. David needs help, but he also seeks mercy. He knows that he is not always in the right.

> Lord, do not rebuke me in your anger
>   or discipline me in your wrath.
> Have mercy on me, Lord, for I am faint;
>   heal me, Lord, for my bones are in agony.
> My soul is in deep anguish.
>   How long, Lord, how long?
> ~Psalm 6:1–3

Speaking of trouble. David not only prays for help and mercy, he examines his troubles in the presence of God. All is not easy, and all is not well.

> But I am a worm and not a man,
>   scorned by everyone, despised by the people.
> All who see me mock me;
>   they hurl insults, shaking their heads.
> "He trusts in the Lord," they say,
>   "let the Lord rescue him.
> Let him deliver him,
>   since he delights in him."
> ~Psalm 22:6–8

Innocence and confidence. Even though he knows his failings, David is quick to assert his fundamental faithfulness. He has confidence in his relationship with God.

> You, God, are my God,
>   earnestly I seek you;
> I thirst for you,

    my whole being longs for you,
    in a dry and parched land
        where there is no water…

    On my bed I remember you;
        I think of you through the watches of the night.
    Because you are my help,
        I sing in the shadow of your wings.
    I cling to you;
        your right hand upholds me.
    ~Psalm 63:1, 6–8

Love and praise. In spite of trouble and sin, David's love for God wells up like a spring. His relationship is not fundamentally transactional; it's personal and grateful. David lives by grace.

    My heart, O God, is steadfast,
        my heart is steadfast;
        I will sing and make music.
    Awake, my soul!
        Awake, harp and lyre!
        I will awaken the dawn.

    I will praise you, Lord, among the nations;
        I will sing of you among the peoples.
    For great is your love, reaching to the heavens;
        your faithfulness reaches to the skies.
    ~Psalm 57:7–10

* *

From reading his psalms, we learn that David perceives God as a living person. This God isn't far off; he is as close as David's breath. David trusts the goodness of God. Even when he complains or questions God—which he often does—he does so in faith. He believes in God's fairness and his love—and he wants to see it. He believes in God's power to make things right, and when it doesn't happen, he wants to know why.

In the faith that David demonstrated, such demands are permitted. More, they are encouraged. Plenty of people want to know why they don't experience the security, protection, rescue, love, and blessing that the Bible describes. They want an explanation! They can't find a better way to address those complaints to God than through the Psalms.

We read plenty of poetry elsewhere in the Old Testament, but most of the emotion is God's. God gets angry; God shows tenderness; God is indignant; God loves. David's poetry stands apart: distinctly human-focused, even while it is God-centered. This is how *we* feel.

Judging by his prayers, David is not focused on accumulating money or power, nor about winning admirers. He is not about building great monuments or celebrating his achievements. David's passion is for God, whom he loves, and for God's plans in the world. He wants to flourish in God's kingdom, praising God and enjoying him. As king, he wants to protect and strengthen his people so they can do the same.

David taught these passions to Israel in his psalms. As a result, the Bible as a whole orbits his fundamental conception of a personal God who relates to us lovingly and honestly. Without the Psalms, the Bible would be a very different book.

* *

Jesus, the Son of David, was not a poet. To the best of our knowledge, he never wrote anything. Nevertheless, he used words powerfully to lead his people. Like David, he shaped Israel by his words. He shapes us.

Jesus typically taught using parables. These are simple stories or similes that are easily remembered. They don't appear very impressive from a literary point of view. But have you tried to make up one of your own? Try expressing some important truth in a parable, and I guarantee you will grow in your appreciation of Jesus' genius. Parables are like cartwheels: they look easy until you try to do one. Jesus seemingly spun them out effortlessly. It is remarkable how many of his parables have become imbedded in general consciousness, e.g., the Prodigal Son and the Good Samaritan. People who have never touched a Bible know these characters.

We don't have many examples of Jesus' prayers—certainly nothing like as many as David left us. The only long prayer is John 17. Like David, Jesus talks to God the Father in a simple, direct way, as though to a friend or an ally. "Righteous Father, though the world does not know you, I know you." (John 17:25) Jesus speaks openly about his situation (he is about to die), and he asks God to act on his behalf. Jesus speaks to God from within a very intimate and personal relationship. He prays like David.

Jesus' prayers drew even closer to David's on the day of his death. In Gethsemane, he prayed, "My Father, if it is possible, may this cup be taken from me. Yet not as I will, but as you will." (Matthew 26:39) Can you hear David's voice in that?

Three short prayers are recorded from the cross.

> "Father, forgive them; for they do not know what they are doing." (Luke 23:34)

> "My God, my God, why have you forsaken me?" (Matthew 27:46; Mark 15:34)

> "Father, into your hands I commit my spirit." (Luke 23:46)

As with David's prayers, these all show a personal encounter with a living God, filled with powerful emotion. As a matter of fact, the last two prayers *are* David's prayers. "My God, my God, why have you forsaken me?" is the first verse of Psalm 22, and "Father, into your hands I commit my spirit," is the fifth verse of Psalm 31.

Both of these Psalms deal with David under attack from his enemies. They juxtapose trust in God with the horrors of betrayal and slander and death. Jesus, a devout Jew who prayed the Psalms all his life, was praying these prayers on the cross. Out loud, he spoke only one verse of each, but he surely knew the whole prayer by heart.

Psalm 22 is particularly of interest, because "My God, my God, why have you forsaken me?" is often cited as Jesus' cry of inconceivable despair. Could God really abandon him?

If you know the whole psalm, however, the message shifts. Psalm 22 details horrifying violence that sounds like a lynching, but then it suddenly turns. Without explanation, praise breaks out. Rescue has come, and the benefits have spread to the poor. The whole world is drawn into praise. Jesus' cry of despair on the cross, as he knew very well, leads on to rescue and praise.

Short as they are, Jesus' prayers from the cross are an indelible part of his legacy. Every Good Friday, they are remembered again. Through his example of prayer, Jesus shapes his people still.

* *

As a writer, I find it endlessly interesting to learn how other writers work. Do they walk around the room and then sit down and rip off a paragraph? Do they write sentences in their head before committing them to paper? I wish I could ask David. Did he stay up late at night to write? Did he set aside an hour each morning? Did he scribble when he was inspired? Did he try out lyrics while playing his lyre, and only later write them down?

In whatever way he did it, he put considerable time and energy into it. Poetry of this quality does not happen by accident.

For anyone who aspires to leadership, the lesson is obvious. Power and money and management skills are not your most powerful tools. Words are: words that are creative, and personal, and beautiful. David ruled Israel with his words.

I admit this is sweet territory for me: I'm a writer. Of course I value words. Let me remind you, however, that everybody uses words. You may not be much of a writer, but you make conversation every day. You communicate love to your loved ones, strategy to your co-workers, sympathy and interest to everybody. There is an art to doing it well.

I came late to understanding the importance of verbal communication. I really thought that when you talked, you just opened your mouth and used any words that came to mind. If I told a story, my affect was flat, and I made no attempt to draw my listeners in. If I told a joke, I often muffed the punchline. I gave no thought to my words.

A number of friends changed me. One was Philip Yancey: when he told a story, he put his whole heart into it. Listening to him, I began to think that I might have more influence in the office if I put some effort into my verbal communication. I began to actually try to tell a story, or make a point, in a more compelling way.

Then, I met the woman who would become my wife. Popie was by far the most positive communicator I had ever met. She encouraged and complimented and admired everybody. She wasn't a flatterer, but she had a way of seizing small attributes and holding them up for appreciation. I saw firsthand that Popie's positive regard helped people become their better selves. Her words were actually powerful—much more so than the cutting wit or the trenchant observation I might favor. I began to try to compliment others as she did, admiring their best traits. It felt very awkward—it wasn't my style—but I found that I could do it, and that with practice, it became easier.

The power of words! Once you start really listening to the way people talk, you see how much business, and family, and church, and classroom, and even watching sports together are influenced by the (often thoughtless) ways that people talk to each other. When one person starts deliberately changing the tone, it can have a huge influence.

If you aren't good with words, you can get help. Most schools offer speech classes. You can even take classes on how to tell a joke. (Google it; you'll see.) Toastmasters is an extremely effective organization helping people improve their public presentations.

The power of words, though, isn't just a skill you learn like coding. It's a skill that expresses your soul. It's a way of spreading kindness and concern. It extends the fruit of the Spirit: love, joy, peace, kindness, gentleness and self-control. It communicates wisdom. Most of this happens informally, in personal interactions. Just because it's not rated on job evaluations, don't think it lacks significance. As the Bible puts it: "The tongue has the power of life and death, and those who love it will eat its fruit." (Proverbs 18:21)

As king, David held the power of life and death over his subjects. As army commander, he dealt in death. His greatest power was for life, however, not death. Life was in his words, in the deep, beautiful prayers that taught Israel the meaning of a personal relationship with God. Long after David was gone, his words survived. His beloved nation lost battles and experienced national disintegration and exile, but they survived on David's prayers. He taught Jews and Christians how to pray. To join in those prayers is to capture a bit of David's success.

Follow the story to Jesus, and you meet a man who will not call on his army to save his life. He heals; he does not kill. His power lies in the connection to God the Father, all in words: he follows God's direction, he speaks the word of God. His is the purest power we know.

QUESTION FOR MEDITATION

What words inspire you? Have you memorized them?
Do you sing them?

Psalm 51; 2 Samuel 11, 12

9. MIDLIFE

The crisis begins with a failing everybody can relate to. David doesn't feel like going to work.

This isn't characteristic. David's primary work responsibility is leading the army. He is not only a skilled fighter, he is an eager one. From the days when he jumped at the chance to take on Goliath, he has always been fearless and ready to lead in battle. But not now. Springtime is the usual time for armies to take the field, but on this occasion, David stays home. He sends Joab, his top general, into battle with the Ammonites while he remains in Jerusalem.

Perhaps he is depressed. He has accomplished everything he set out to do. He outlasted Saul, he defeated the Philistines, he united the tribes, he built his palace in Jerusalem. The adrenaline rush is over. David has no more mountains to climb. God has turned down his bid to build a temple. Perhaps his future looks like a dull gray haze—more of the same, forever.

You know how this comes out, don't you? A bored and restless man has ways of finding trouble. On a sleepless night, walking on the roof overlooking the city, David looks down to see a beautiful woman at her bath. The moonlight gleams on her wet skin, and he is aroused. She is the wife of one of his bravest fighters, Uriah, who just happens to be on the battlefield—where David should be. David sends for Bathsheba, and they spend the night.

It's very unlikely that anybody will question David's adultery with Bathsheba. The servants know all about it, and others probably do, too. Nobody says a word. You don't question royalty. Anyway, men do this kind of thing. (So people have been saying, excusing it, for three thousand years.)

In the ancient world, women are disposable, and kings are the ultimate disposers. During the seven years David spent in Hebron, he had six sons by six different wives. When he settled in Jerusalem, he added more wives and concubines, so many and so inconsequential they are not even considered worth naming. (2 Samuel 4:13) Did Bathsheba have a choice when the king summoned her to his bedroom? Probably not in any meaningful way. A powerful man, a powerless woman, and a summons that does not contemplate a refusal. In our world, we have a name for this: sexual assault.

Later Bathsheba sends a message: "I am pregnant." That does pose a problem, though not a very big one. The pregnancy can be bluffed through. If you read your European history, you know that there are lots of affairs and lots of illicit babies among the nobility, but somehow, royal life goes on. I presume David could leave it to Uriah to figure out what to do with a wife who gives birth to a child who doesn't look like him, born nine months after his time on the battlefield. Uriah won't mention it to the king, if he is wise.

David evidently can't quite imagine facing down Uriah that way, however. Maybe his own self-image as a righteous man won't let him take that route. After all, he has written songs proclaiming his personal integrity. He prefers to try to hide what he has done. He sets out to deceive Uriah by inviting him home for a visit from the front. That way, Uriah can sleep with his wife, and when the baby comes, never be sure it isn't his.

(And by the way, in inviting Uriah home, David demonstrates his deepest feelings for Bathsheba. He doesn't plan to keep her. She is disposable.)

It turns out that Uriah is too loyal to go home to his wife; he feels that a soldier shouldn't sleep so comfortably while his comrades suffer on the battlefield. Instead, he unrolls his sleeping bag on the front steps. Perplexed by a man with more honor than he, David is thrust into a much worse cover-up. He arranges with Joab to send Uriah forward into an exposed position on the battlefield and then suddenly withdraw behind him. The plan works. Uriah is killed. The subsequent exchange between David and Joab is extremely cold-blooded. "David told the messenger [who brought word of Uriah's death], 'Say this to Joab: "Don't let this upset you; the sword devours one as well as another. Press the attack against the city and destroy it." Say this to encourage Joab.'" (2 Samuel 11:25)

Who is this cold fish? Is this the man who wrote, in Psalm 7,

> LORD my God, if I have done this
>   and there is guilt on my hands—
> if I have repaid my ally with evil
>   or without cause have robbed my foe—
> then let my enemy pursue and overtake me;
>   let him trample my life to the ground
>   and make me sleep in the dust.

Or in Psalm 26,

> Vindicate me, LORD,
>   for I have led a blameless life…

He waits for Bathsheba's mourning period to be over and then brings her to the palace to bear his son. Still nobody says a word to him, though surely many talk about it privately. "But the thing David had done displeased the Lord."

* *

In a remarkable essay entitled, "Your Professional Decline is Coming (Much) Sooner Than You Think," Arthur C. Brooks tells of a nighttime airline flight in which he overheard a whispered conversation.

> "It's not *true* that no one needs you anymore."
>   These words came from an elderly woman sitting behind me on a late-night flight from Los Angeles to Washington, D.C. The plane was dark and quiet. A man I assumed to be her husband murmured almost inaudibly in response, something to the effect of "I wish I was dead."
>   Again, the woman: "Oh, stop saying that."

I didn't mean to eavesdrop, but couldn't help it. I listened with morbid fascination, forming an image of the man in my head as they talked. I imagined someone who had worked hard all his life in relative obscurity, someone with unfulfilled dreams—perhaps of the degree he never attained, the career he never pursued, the company he never started.

At the end of the flight, as the lights switched on, I finally got a look at the desolate man. I was shocked. I recognized him—he was, and still is, world-famous. Then in his mid-80s, he was beloved as a hero for his courage, patriotism, and accomplishments many decades ago.

As he walked up the aisle of the plane behind me, other passengers greeted him with veneration. Standing at the door of the cockpit, the pilot stopped him and said, "Sir, I have admired you since I was a little boy." The older man—apparently wishing for death just a few minutes earlier—beamed with pride at the recognition of his past glories.

According to Brooks, researchers find that on average, people in creative careers grow in success and productivity for the first twenty years of their work. They then begin an inevitable decline. If they draw emotional support from their achievements—as successful people usually do—they may become depressed by their career trajectory.

Brooks learned that it's not unusual for somebody famous to feel desperate. When they reach middle age, their success often diminishes, or they begin to see that it doesn't complete their lives the way they expected. That can provoke a crisis.

Perhaps that happened to David. He had been leading a military force for approximately 20 years, much of it under great stress. Through long years in exile, he must have thought and prayed about what he would do as king. Now he had done it all, and more. He had secured and unified Israel as a nation. His songs, we may assume, were being sung all over Israel. He lived in a palace. He had wives. He had children. All this must have given him joy—for a time. Did he then wonder: is that all there is?

Professor Stephen Prothero writes, "A few years ago an academic journal devoted an entire issue to one of my books. I was flattered, but when the issue arrived I had no desire to read it. I emailed a friend about my disinterest, which surprised me. 'Of course!' she responded. 'The only thing your ego does is say "you're great" and "you stink," over and over again, in internally referential and self-perpetuating loops... Any form of criticism is a version of "you stink," and any form of praise is another version of the same message, since "you're great" implies you would stink if you weren't great in that way.'"

New York Times columnist David Brooks says something similar about his experience of success: "*Career success is fulfilling.* This is the lie we foist on the young. In their tender years we put the most privileged of them inside a college admissions process that puts achievement and status anxiety at the center of their lives. That begins advertising's lifelong mantra — if you make it, life will be good.

"Everybody who has actually tasted success can tell you that's not true. I remember when the editor of my first book called to tell me it had made the best-seller list. It felt like ... nothing. It was external to me."

* *

What do you do when success doesn't satisfy? Arthur Brooks says that someone facing midlife decline may want to restart their career, perhaps de-emphasizing work that requires fast, nimble thinking and long working hours and instead taking up work that rewards wisdom, such as teaching or mentoring. He also mentions the value of developing spiritual qualities that have been neglected during the rush of a successful career.

David evidently does neither. He stays home from the battle, but then falls into temptation with his neighbor's wife. Unable to admit his failings and let go of his reputation for righteousness, he murders Bath-sheba's husband. He's cold-blooded. There's no indication in the Bible that he repents in the least—until the prophet Nathan appears.

We don't know where Nathan came from or how he got in the front door. He is a nobody, like all the prophets. But he is a brave man. Without a shred of human support, he strides into David's court and launches into a story about a poor man with a beloved pet lamb. A rich man snatched that lamb to feed it to a guest, though he had plenty of lambs of his own.

David must listen to sob stories every day. Kings function as judges, the last court of appeal for those who feel cheated or abused. Nathan tells the lamb story as a case for David to adjudicate. It catches David's attention, maybe because he himself cared for sheep. Maybe because he spent so many years running from Saul that he feels for the underdog. At any rate, he reacts strongly. Burning with anger, he tells Nathan that the rich man deserves to die, "because he did such a thing and had no pity."

Nathan the storyteller suddenly changes shape, becoming the prosecuting attorney. He cries out, "You are the man!" After all God gave him, he tells David, he "despised the word of the Lord by doing what is evil in his eyes." Since he killed Uriah, "the sword will never depart from your house." Furthermore, someone close to David, within his own household, will steal his wives and sleep with them in public. "You did it in secret, but I will do this thing in broad daylight before all Israel." (2 Samuel 12:12)

It is terrible and humiliating to be caught in the act, in public, without prior warning. Take all 100 members of the U.S. Senate, consider any President you care to, add any governor or corporate CEO, and ask yourself how they would respond to such a hijacking. I am sure they would fight back like tigers. Nobody gets to a powerful position by humbly accepting blame.

King David could easily have Nathan killed, or at least thrown out on his ear. He does not. He takes in what Nathan says—words nobody else dared to even hint. David says for all to hear, "I have sinned against the Lord."

It may be the greatest moment of David's life. He takes responsibility. He recognizes that he has grievously harmed other people and that in doing so, he violated his relationship to God.

Few leaders are willing to come clean that way. President Richard Nixon famously proclaimed to a TV audience, "I am not a crook."

President Bill Clinton, when asked why he said of Monica Lewinsky, "There's nothing going on between us," claimed, "It depends upon what the meaning of the word 'is' is."

David does not try to weasel out of it. He doesn't claim any mitigating circumstances. He just takes the rap: "I have sinned against the Lord."

Nathan responds, "The Lord has taken away your sin. You are not going to die."

Die! That word must land like a brick on a birthday cake. Could the king be executed for his crimes? I wonder whether the proper legal consequences had even crossed David's mind. People in power usually think themselves above all that.

Nathan does not suggest that forgiveness will obliterate all consequences. David will not die, but the baby born out of his unfaithfulness will.

When the baby falls ill, David acts as though his own life is at stake. "He pleaded with God for the child. He fasted and went into his house and spent the nights lying on the ground. The elders of his household stood beside him to get him up from the ground but he refused, and he would not eat any food with them." (2 Samuel 12:16–17) The death of any child is a heartbreak as deep as a well, but something more is involved here. David realizes the depth of what he has done. An innocent child is suffering and dying for David's sins. Probably David thinks, *I wish I could die. It should be me.*

Psalm 51 records David's repentance.

> Deliver me from the guilt of bloodshed, O God,
>   you who are God my Savior,
>   and my tongue will sing of your righteousness.
> Open my lips, Lord,
>   and my mouth will declare your praise.
> You do not delight in sacrifice, or I would bring it;
>   you do not take pleasure in burnt offerings.
> My sacrifice, O God, is a broken spirit.

We see and hear David's regret. What we don't see is anybody sharing his pain. We don't see anybody praying for him or with him. Maybe Nathan acted as his pastor, but we don't know anything about that. As far as we can tell, David bears the agony alone.

All his life he has been alone, except for the few moments he spent with Jonathan, who is dead. He grew up disregarded by his family. He spent his early years in exile, running for his life. Then he became a militia leader and a king. He was in charge of men; he was never a peer.

It's true of a lot of successful people. It takes time and patience to keep up with people, to remember to call them, to get together for lunch, to go camping together. If you're on the fast flight to winning, you don't have bandwidth for that.

You also find social barriers. The CEO of the company can't be an equal with his Vice President. He can't pal around with him—not genuinely. He can't share his weakness or his doubts.

Part of the penalty for success is the pain of isolation. David experiences it now. He has no social equals. Many people want to be close, but only to use him, and he knows that. He has kept his distance from everybody—or has allowed that distance to be kept—and now he pays the price. At this moment of supreme personal loss, he has no one who can provide comfort or counsel.

At the end of a week, the child's heart stops. He is dead. To everyone's surprise, David takes the news calmly. He gets up and goes about his business. He comforts his wife Bathsheba; she becomes pregnant again and gives birth to a boy named Solomon. David goes back to his job, leading the army and successfully attacking enemy raiders. It appears that all is well, that life has gone on. The story is not really over, though. In fact, it has barely begun.

* *

Arthur Brooks tells the story of Charles Darwin, the great biologist who first theorized the deep history of living things. His career began when he was 22 years old and shipped out on the HMS *Beagle* to do biological research in South America. He returned to England five years later to great acclaim. Over the next 23 years, he developed his theories of natural selection and evolution, culminating with the bestselling *On the Origin of Species*. He was 50 years old and world famous. From that point on, however, his research hit a wall, and he made little progress. This, along with health problems, contributed to a growing depression. Brooks quotes a letter Darwin wrote to a friend late in life: "I have not the heart or strength at my age to begin any investigation lasting years, which is the only thing which I enjoy."

One of the greatest scientists of all time, extraordinarily acclaimed during his own lifetime, might have echoed the man on the airplane. Or he might have echoed David.

Brooks tells another story of midlife decline. Johann Sebastian Bach is now regarded as one of the greatest composers of all time. He grew up in a very musical family, and early on gained a reputation as a master organist—which was a preeminent musical skill in an era where most music was church music, and every church of any size featured an organ. Bach could play the organ like nobody else. His skill as a composer—

he wrote thousands of pieces—won him great fame as well. He was as famous as any musician in Europe—a rock star, in today's language.

But in his later years, his fame greatly diminished. Musical styles changed, and he was left behind. Rather than becoming embittered or depressed, as Darwin apparently did, or acting out a midlife crisis, as David did, Bach changed direction. He had chased fame all over Germany, but now he settled down in Leipzig, where he raised his large family. In the final years of his life, he devoted his attention to two works that made no splash at all: *The Art of the Fugue*, which was meant to instruct in the techniques of baroque music, and the *Mass in B Minor*, which brought together his best choral pieces for one exalted work devoted to God. (Bach inscribed all his musical works with *Soli Deo gloria*—Glory to God alone. "The aim and final end of all music," he once said, "should be none other than the glory of God and the refreshment of the soul.")

The *Mass in B Minor* was never performed in Bach's lifetime, and *The Art of the Fugue* was not even completed before his death. Both are now revered as among the greatest works of music of all time, but during Bach's life, they were unknown. When fame deserted Bach, he did not chase it. Rather he devoted himself to family, to teaching, and to compositions that he deemed significant, regardless of their popularity. He died loved and respected—though less famous than he had been.

* *

Like Bach, like Darwin, and like David, David's Son Jesus was certainly an early success. An unknown from a rural town, a carpenter's son with no rabbinic pedigree, he swiftly became nationally famous both as a healer and as a teacher. Crowds followed him everywhere. His disciples adored him.

As the years went by, however, opposition arose. He became a polarizing figure, with some in the religious establishment seeking to do away with him. What had come effortlessly now became difficult and dangerous. Many of his followers deserted him when they realized what a rigorous message he preached. (John 6:66)

But loss of popularity did not provoke a midlife crisis. Jesus wasn't after personal success; he lived as a man for others.

David and the Son of David offer quite a contrast. David was an extraordinary leader: charismatic, skilled at political feats needed for unifying the quarrelsome tribes, militarily brilliant, courageous, God-centered, verbally gifted, emotionally in touch: and in the final analysis, almost completely conventional. His gifts were bent toward typical achievement: military success, political success, personal success. He got it, and he squandered it. He threw it away on sex and then on a sickening attempt at preserving his reputation.

The Son of David, Jesus, was also an extraordinary leader: charismatic, a deep thinker who could use words to penetrate minds, God-centered, verbally gifted, courageous, emotionally in touch, spiritually powerful: and in the final analysis, unlike anyone you have ever known. His gifts were bent to a cause that other leaders, political or religious, couldn't understand. Sin and death took him down to the dark place of suffering. He never hesitated. He knew what he was called to do. He stuck with it to the end.

Nobody stays at the top of the mountain forever. There is always a climb-down. Disappointment and disillusionment are part of the journey of success and failure. True success requires learning to adjust and find new meaning, rather than spoiling it all with your frustration.

Be like Jesus, not David. Cultivate friends. Seek wisdom, seek counsel. Cultivate humility and gratefulness. Double down on your calling. Rethink it; find ways to devote yourself to it anew. Don't let yourself be bored. Live for others.

QUESTION FOR REFLECTION

If you achieve everything you dream of, will you be satisfied?

10. GUILT PARALYSIS

The sons of kings are naturally rivals. Only one of them can inherit the crown, and it is not unknown for the leading candidate to kill off his competitors.

Take Richard III, who became king of England in 1483. He was born eleventh of 12 children to Richard, Duke of York, a powerful nobleman in a turbulent and violent time. Richard was just a boy when his father was killed in battle, fighting over who would be king. Richard and his brother George were sent abroad for safety, then returned to England when their oldest brother was crowned King Edward IV.

For more than 20 years Richard was an ambitious but loyal supporter of his brother the king. When Edward IV died (of natural causes—unusually for that era), his 12-year-old son, Edward V, succeeded him. Richard was named his Lord Protector. He and a small army escorted the young king to the Tower of London, where royalty traditionally stayed while they waited for coronation. His younger brother went there with him: two young boys with all the expectations of England riding on their shoulders.

While the young king waited to be crowned, a clergyman asserted to Richard that young Edward's parents had not been properly married; therefore, he was a bastard and could not become king. Days later, a sermon was preached in front of St. Paul's Cathedral repeating the story and calling for Richard to become king instead. Shortly thereafter, a citizen's petition spontaneously called for the same thing. Soon, Richard was crowned. The would-be king Edward V and his younger brother were never seen again.

* *

The sons of kings not only are naturally rivals, they often grow up spoiled. No one dares to correct them, and their parents are too busy. Such parenting failures were a problem among Israel's leaders. Eli had bad sons. Samuel had bad sons. Saul, remarkably, had at least one very good son, Jonathan. David's sons, unfortunately, revert to the norm.

This isn't, however, a story about David's bad sons; it's a story about David and his guilty conscience. Guilt is a terrible thing. It makes people act irrationally, sometimes weak and unable to pass judgment, sometimes hyper-moralistic, projecting their own failings onto others. On the path to success and failure, people often acquire a guilty conscience. It distorts their behavior. For those in leadership, it's particularly destructive. So it was for David.

David's oldest son, Amnon, fell in love with his half-sister, Tamar. The Bible describes a classic infatuation, with Amnon making himself sick with frustrated longing. He sees her around the palace, and every time he does, he feels squeamish with love. He cannot marry his sister, of course, which makes his infatuation worse. His cousin Jonadab notices how out of sorts Amnon is and suggests that he play sick and lure the tender-hearted Tamar into his apartment.

Amnon takes the advice. He makes a show of his pretend illness. When David comes to see his "sick" son, Amnon begs the king to send Tamar with some homemade cookies.

She brings the cookies, but Amnon throws a tantrum and won't eat. He orders everybody else out of the apartment and then coyly invites Tamar into his bedroom. Naively, she follows. When they are alone, he grabs her wrist and pulls her toward him. "Sleep with me!" he cries, and will not let go.

She begs him. She tries to reason with him, she warns him, she pleads with him to spare her the shame. He ignores her cries, forces her onto the bed, and rapes her.

Afterward, he experiences a classic emotional reversal, becoming repulsed by her. He rudely orders Tamar to get out. She begs piteously to stay. Perhaps, she pleads pathetically, the king might accept their relationship if they ask for special permission to marry.

Amnon won't listen. He calls his attendant and has him drag Tamar out of the apartment and lock the door. Weeping and in distress, she tears her fancy dress, then runs to a fireplace and rubs ashes into her hair, screaming at the top of her voice.

Her brother Absalom hears her cries. Understanding instantly what has happened, he comes to put his arms around her. Absalom holds her until she calms down. He tells her not to worry; he will take care of her. Tamar goes home with him, to live with him.

* *

Amnon's treatment of his sister combines abuse, deceit, incest, and rape. Nothing could be more awful. When King David gets wind of it, he is naturally furious. Yet he does nothing. As the head of government, and as Amnon and Tamar's father, he is obligated to respond, but he does not. It's the first sign that he is paralyzed by guilt.

David must not have slept much those nights. How can he condemn Amnon? He has done worse. He feels for his son.

Absalom feels no such ambivalence. He is a pretty boy who inherited his father's confidence, the cocksure self-certainty that doesn't care what others think. His confidence isn't anchored by God, as his father's was. He stews on his hatred for his brother, biding his time. Eventually, he lures Amnon to an out-of-town party. When Amnon is tipsy, he murders him. Absalom then skips town to go live with his mother's family in Geshur, a tiny kingdom east of the Sea of Galilee. He will be safe from arrest there.

Absalom remains in exile for three years, during which time David mourns for him every day. Fathers love their sons, and that love doesn't diminish when the sons do wrong. Does David now perversely see himself in Absalom? Does he see them both, weirdly, as victims of their own failings? Emotions are hard to read, but Joab, the army chief, characteristically takes a pragmatic approach. He sees that David wants his son back, but that David needs an excuse. Joab coaches a woman to tell David a story—shades of Nathan—about her two sons. One killed the other; she fears that her only remaining son will be killed in retribution, and then she will have no son at all. When David hears this pathetic tale, he promises to make sure nobody hurts her remaining son. Once she has the promise, she turns the case on David. Isn't he punishing his own son for doing the same thing?

David recognizes Joab's hand in the woman's manipulation, but he is—as Joab knew—eager to be manipulated. He tells Joab to bring Absalom home. His only punishment is that David will refuse to see him. This at least poses as a punishment. In reality, David is punishing himself. He remains tormented by his own failings, and so refuses to treat himself to a reunion. He is the one who longs to see his son.

After two years, Absalom grows impatient with this treatment. He wants to be recognized in the king's palace, so he calls Joab to see him. Joab does not come. He calls a second time, with no answer. Characteristically, he sets Joab's field on fire. That gets Joab to come.

"Why have I come from Geshur?" Absalom asks him angrily. "It would be better for me if I were still there. I want to see the king's face, and if I am guilty of anything, let him put me to death." Absalom has yet to show the slightest hint of repentance. In his mind, his brother got what he deserved, and he, Absalom, is the victim.

When Joab repeats this to David, he relents. Longing to be forgiven himself, he eagerly forgives Absalom. When the son arrives at the palace, he embraces his father. The murder is forgotten.

* *

I have asked myself how I would feel toward my son if he murdered his brother. I find that I can't begin to imagine it. It's an unthinkable horror. Compound that with a deep, grinding guilt for your own act of murder, and you get paralysis. That is how it affected David. He didn't know what he should do to Absalom, so he did nothing. The wound went untreated.

In the Broadway musical *Hamilton*, Lin-Manuel Miranda has a song, "It's Quiet Uptown," about Alexander Hamilton and his wife Eliza trying to go on living after their son Philip died in a duel. Hamilton feels guilty: he supplied the guns his son took to the duel. He himself is a hothead who has fought in duels; he surely inspired his son to do the same. He never thought that his lovely son could die. Now he deals with a loss that's simply unimaginable.

> There are moments that the words don't reach
> There is suffering too terrible to name
> You hold your child as tight as you can
> And push away the unimaginable

Unimaginable. That's what David must feel his life has become. One son raped his sister; the other murdered his brother. It's simply unimaginable. So is David's unfathomable choice to sleep with Bathsheba and then murder her husband. He could never do such a thing. He's too good a man. It's unimaginable. Yet it is so. And he is stuck, frozen in the unimaginable.

* *

The closest I come to understanding David's position is to think about drug addiction. I volunteer in a drug and alcohol rehab program, so I know lots of people who are addicted. To a lesser extent, I know their families. Of course, many don't really have families anymore. Many have burned bridges with nearly everybody: family, friends, church members, teachers.

That happens through repeated acts of betrayal. Money disappears. Televisions disappear. Prescription drugs disappear. Cars get wrecked. Ambulances rush to the hospital pursued by fearful prayers. Fathers shout with fury. Mothers lie awake dreading a call. People can stand only so much. After one too many violations, they don't answer the phone. They tell their brother or sister or son or daughter not to come home any more.

The people who love addicts experience a terrible helplessness, and usually a terrible guilt.

Writer David Sheff published an article in the *New York Times* detailing his son Nick's addiction to methamphetamines. (The article was later expanded into a book and then a movie, both entitled *Beautiful Boy*.) It's a gritty, emotional account of a father's desperate attempts to save his son's life. Sheff goes through repeated highs and lows as his son enters rehab, pledges that he will never use drugs again, and then relapses. Again and again the cycle repeats. Hope alternates with despair. Sheff fears his son may die if he keeps using. Desperate to help him, he spends extraordinary amounts of money and devotes huge amounts of time, all in vain. He loves Nick desperately, but he's not accomplishing anything.

Al-Anon, the organization that supports the family members of addicts, refers to the "three Cs" that every relative must absorb: "You didn't cause it, you can't cure it, you can't control it." Sheff learns to accept the last two: he can't control his son's drug use, and he can't cure his addiction. He's not so sure about the first one. "Part of me feels solely responsible—if only his mother and I had stayed together; if only she and I had lived in the same city after the divorce and had a joint-custody arrangement that was easier on him; if only I had set stricter limits; if only I had been more consistent."

He is plagued by memories of his own youthful drug use, which he told Nick about. Did that subtly encourage Nick to think that all would be well if he used drugs, that there would be no consequences? Father and son even smoked marijuana together. At the time, Sheff took it all lightly, but now that he sees the consequences of addiction working themselves out in Nick's life, he's tormented by guilt. "People outside can vilify me," he writes. "They can criticize me. They can blame me. [Nick] can. But nothing they can say or do is worse than what I do to myself every day. 'You didn't cause it.' I do not believe it."

Sheff threw everything he had into making things right for Nick. He flirted with co-dependence, the tendency of loved ones to rescue those who are addicted from the consequences of their drug abuse. The desire to help can be a problem, not a cure.

David's case with Absalom is classic co-dependence. He feels guilty for the example he set for his son. So he shields Absalom from the consequences of his behavior. He never warns him, he never sets boundaries, he never punishes him. He can't bear to see his son suffer. He is unmanned by his guilt, and in the process, he creates a monster.

* *

Jesus, David's Son, lived his entire ministry on intimate terms with Judas, a man who (as Jesus knew) was as unreliable and dangerous as Absalom. Jesus trusted Judas, choosing him among the original 12 disciples and making him treasurer of the traveling group. Judas put on a good act, pretending he was genuinely concerned for the poor, but when the pressure was on, he only cared about himself. More, he was willing to betray Jesus—to turn him in to the authorities—in return for cash.

We don't know exactly what went through Judas' mind. We do know that betrayal was his idea. Nobody enticed him. He approached the chief priests, asking what they would give for information. After being paid, he carried on following Jesus, right up to the Passover dinner that they celebrated together.

The gospel accounts make very clear that Jesus knew what Judas was up to. In view of that, it's remarkable to note how he handled him during the Passover meal, the Last Supper. Talking one-on-one over the dinner table, he let Judas know that he knew his secret. In fact, he urged Judas to go and do what he had to do—right to the point where Judas got up and left the meal. The other disciples thought he left on an errand, but Judas knew that Jesus knew his true errand.

Jesus didn't try to stop him. He loved Judas, and he gave Judas every opportunity to back out of his betrayal. He did everything but try to control him.

Jesus looked Judas in the eye. By contrast, David could not bring up murder with Absalom even after the fact. He had to pretend that all was well.

Could Judas have stopped short? Yes, most certainly. He did not have to betray Jesus. When Judas saw that Jesus would be executed, Matthew reports that he was sorry for what he had done. He tried to give the money back. When the priests wouldn't take it, he threw the money on the floor and went out to kill himself.

Jesus never stopped loving him. There is a poignant moment when Judas found Jesus on the Mount of Olives in the middle of the night. Judas had promised to embrace Jesus when he located him in the darkness, so the police would know whom to arrest. Jesus asked, "Judas, is it with a kiss that you are betraying the Son of Man?"

Unlike David, Jesus spoke directly to Judas, showing that he knew exactly what was up, that he was not deceived. He warned him. He told Judas that rather than do what he planned, it would be better if he were never born. If David had spoken to his son that way, he might have stopped. Absalom might have become human again. He might have lived. And David's accomplishments in building a strong and united kingdom might also have lived.

If David had spoken to his son that way, he himself might have confronted his own guilt. Instead of letting it fester, he might have brought it out into the open and experienced healing.

Somebody might say that David had dealt with his guilt. Nathan had pronounced him forgiven in the name of God. He had written his confession publicly in Psalm 51. He had suffered the death of his baby son.

Yet he suffered alone. He never talked. At some deeper level, he evidently remained unforgiven in his own soul. He carried guilt that kept him from dealing plainly and factually with his sons' guilt. I wonder how much guilt afflicts people we know. I wonder how much dysfunction in the church, in business, in family, and in community rises out of guilty consciences, sometimes overreacting to others' failings and sometimes frozen by them, unable to respond in a human way.

It may not seem that guilt has anything to do with success or failure. Lots of successful people live wickedly and seem to prosper all the more. I don't believe it, though. We can deny guilt but we cannot make it go away; and guilt will always burrow into our psyche and make us act cruelly and irrationally, somewhere, somehow. It may not affect our bank account. It will affect our lives and pull us down.

* *

Guilt remains a plague on everyone's life who stores it up and does not confess. I'm not referring to the ritual of confession to a priest. I'm talking about the accountability of friends. It's frank and unfiltered conversation with someone who knows you well, who loves you, who will listen and who can tell you you're forgiven in the name of Jesus.

As previously noted, many successful people don't have such a friend. They are too busy to make them.

Even if they have them, the thought of confessing to a friend scares many people half to death. They have never talked that openly to anybody.

Sin will come. "All have sinned and fall short of the glory of God," as Paul put it in Romans 3:23. Dealing with guilt actually begins long before the sin. It's done by developing the kind of friendship that Jonathan offered David, and that Jesus offered Judas. When his crisis came, David didn't have such a friend, and neither did Judas. Guilt swallowed them both.

QUESTION FOR MEDITATION

Is there some failing in your own life that you have not fully dealt with, and that therefore tips you off balance in your relationships?

11. THE VERY WORST THAT CAN HAPPEN

How bad can life get for a rich, powerful, successful leader? David is about to find out.

His son Absalom is a conniver, obsessed with his own good looks and his fabulous hair. (2 Samuel 14:26) He loves to move around in a chariot with 50 men running ahead of him. (15:1) Now that he is accepted back in the king's court, he becomes a politician, talking in a friendly way to everybody and bad-mouthing his father's administration.

In the nature of things, people complain about the government. Absalom listens to them sympathetically. He meets people as they go into court and says what a pity it is that the government is deaf and dumb. From the king on down, he says, nobody seems to care. He would do it differently, if he were king.

Perhaps Absalom has a point. Perhaps David is depressed and out of sight. How else could Absalom get away with such outrageous behavior? Jerusalem is a small town, and word is bound to get to David—unless he is depressed and withdrawn. Absalom "stole the hearts of the men of Israel." (2 Samuel 15:6) The guilt-frozen David lets him do it, perhaps by not attending to the business of the king.

After four years of this, Absalom goes off to Hebron, where David was first crowned. There he springs his conspiracy to kill his father and take the throne. People respond not with alarm but with excitement. They may have noticed that the government is not as it should be.

When David hears of Absalom's plot, he acts decisively—depressingly so. A messenger brings word that "the hearts of the men of Israel are with Absalom." (2 Samuel 15:13) David, who has been a hero in Israel since he was a young man, who has always been confident in battle, immediately wants to flee. He has no faith in his ability to win a battle against a son who has never led an army. He feels sure that if Absalom catches them, they will all be killed. David has become a very different man from the one who fought Goliath. He has lost all confidence.

David remains frozen by guilt. He has utterly failed as a parent. His own much-loved son is trying to murder him. He can trace it all the way back to his murder of Uriah. He should have died then. Perhaps he wants to die now.

But not quite. David still has enough energy to run away.

Second Samuel's detailed description of David leaving Jerusalem is among the saddest scenes in the Bible. It begins with David pausing on the outskirts of Jerusalem to review his troops. We learn that during his time in Gath, when David fought as a mercenary for the Philistines, he gained the loyalty of 600 Philistine soldiers. They abandoned their homeland to follow him. David now tries to send them back. "You came only yesterday. And today shall I make you wander about with us, when I do not know where I am going?"

The men from Gath refuse to go, so David lets them follow him, accompanied by their families. He has lost everything, it seems, but not the loyalty of his men.

"The whole countryside wept aloud as all the people passed by... David continued up the Mount of Olives, weeping as he went; his head was covered and he was barefoot. All the people with him covered their heads too and were weeping as they went up." (2 Samuel 15:23, 30)

A man named Shimei, from Saul's clan, turns up. "He pelted David and all the king's officials with stones, though all the troops and the special guard were on David's right and left. As he cursed, Shimei said, 'Get out, get out, you man of blood, you scoundrel! The Lord has repaid you for all the blood you shed in the household of Saul, in whose place you have reigned. The Lord has handed the kingdom over to your son Absalom. You have come to ruin because you are a man of blood!'"

One of David's generals gets sick of it. "Why don't I go over and take that guy's head off?" he asks.

But David stops him from killing Shimei. "My son, who is of my own flesh, is trying to take my life. How much more, then, this Benjaminite!

Leave him alone; let him curse, for the Lord has told him to. It may be that the Lord will see my distress and repay me with good for the cursing I am receiving today."

"So David and his men continued along the road while Shimei was going along the hillside opposite him, cursing as he went and throwing stones at him and showering him with dirt. The king and all the people with him arrived at their destination exhausted." (2 Samuel 16:5–14)

Only one scene in the Bible surpasses this one for grief: Jesus carrying his cross out of Jerusalem to Golgotha. He, too, is barefoot, surrounded by weeping people. He, too, is mocked and cursed, making no attempt to defend himself. The Son of David follows David's footsteps, a king rejected by his subjects. In both cases, the king of Israel suffers, is rejected, and faces death at the hand of his own children. Jesus is the Man of Sorrows. So is David.

The difference, of course, is that David is punished for what he has done. He carries his own sins. Jesus makes that slow march of tears carrying the sins of the world. He is innocent, punished for what *we* have done.

* *

Then comes a small piece of wonderful news: David is not abandoned. People come out of the woods to help him, including several non-Israelite neighbors who bring food and bedding and pots. (2 Samuel 17:27–29) David has loyalists in Jerusalem, too, who work to undermine Absalom. David's army remains steadfast. He organizes them into three units—the first sign that he is emerging from his emotional paralysis. David is ready to lead into battle, but his fighters insist he stay behind the lines. "Even if half of us die, they won't care; but you are worth ten thousand of us." (2 Samuel 18:3)

So, as the battle approaches, David stands at the city gate observing the army marching out. He should be encouraging them to fight bravely, but he can't help himself: he is still feeling for his son. He tells his commanders to treat Absalom gently. The whole army hears it. He is emerging from his depression and trying to act like a king, but his heart is still preoccupied with saving his beloved, murderous son.

The battle is joined in a forest and soon spreads over the entire countryside, with great casualties. Famously, Absalom is undone by his wonderful hair. Riding under the branches of an oak, he gets his locks tangled in its branches and ends up hanging in the air while his mule keeps going. When Joab is told that Absalom is dangling, he does not hesitate. Taking three javelins, he plunges them into Absalom's heart. That is the end of Absalom; his army melts away when they realize their leader is dead.

Waiting for news, David doesn't seem to care about victory. All he wants to know is the fate of his son. When he finally learns of Absalom's death, "The king was shaken. He went up to the room over the gateway and wept. As he went, he said: 'O my son Absalom! My son, my son Absalom! If only I had died instead of you—O Absalom, my son, my son!'" (2 Samuel 18:33)

"If only I had died instead of you!" David may be wishing that his army had been overrun and he had been killed, leaving Absalom alive. He loves Absalom so much—and feels so guilt-stricken—that he would sacrifice everything, his own life and his kingdom's life—for the sake of Absalom's survival.

Most likely, his memory is also casting back to his sin with Uriah. He deserved to die then, according to the law. If he had died, executed as he deserved, none of this tragedy would ever have begun.

That is the fantasy entertained by many people thinking of suicide: *If I were gone, everybody would be better off.* In reality, David's death would not clean up the mess he has made. Israel without David would be pathetic and vulnerable, as it had been under Saul. David's sons would fight just as murderously without him as they did with him. His death would merely exchange one set of horrible outcomes for another. No one can sacrifice his life to redeem the world, not even the king.

David's public display of emotion dishonors his army. They ought to celebrate the astonishing military turnaround. Instead, "the victory that day was turned into mourning, because on that day the troops heard it said, 'The king is grieving for his son.' The men stole into the city that day as men steal in who are ashamed when they flee from battle. The king covered his face and cried aloud, 'O my son Absalom! O Absalom, my son, my son!'" (2 Samuel 19:2–4)

Joab—practical, blunt Joab—reads David the riot act, telling him he is humiliating the men who saved his life. "You love those who hate you and hate those who love you. You have made it clear today that the commanders and their men mean nothing to you. I see that you would be pleased if Absalom were alive today and all of us were dead. Now go out and encourage your men. I swear by the Lord that if you don't go out, not a man will be left with you by nightfall." (2 Samuel 19:6–7)

David hears Joab and remembers his duty. He gets up and sits in the gateway to review the army. Soon he will start for Jerusalem, to set his administration back in order.

* *

My junior year of college, I got an unexpected message from home: my father had been put into a mental hospital.

I was undone by the news, so much so that I cannot even remember who called me. It must have been my mother, but I do not recall the sound of her voice. Apparently, I blocked it out; how else would I forget who called me with the most dreadful news I have ever heard? All I remember is terror. I went to my sister's dorm room, not far from mine, and we took in the awful scene together. I think we prayed, haltingly, helplessly, but I cannot really remember that, either. I remember fear. For us in those days, the term "mental illness" was worse than "terminal cancer." As far as we knew, mental hospitals opened their doors like the gates of hell, and nobody ever emerged. I thought I would never see my father again, except as a broken shell.

I had been aware beforehand that my father was struggling. All my life, I had seen him occasionally depressed and withdrawn. He had always been a little obsessive. Mental illness seemed to be a different category, however.

My dad was a pastor, and the church leaders, seeing that he was deeply depressed, had insisted he go for a mental evaluation. My parents felt that the church treated them very badly. In retrospect, I don't believe they did, but when you face the abyss, you don't necessarily see things objectively.

I loved my parents very deeply, but I knew of nothing I could do. My mother didn't tell me much; she just agonized. None of our family knew how to share our feelings. (No doubt that was part of my dad's problem.) We suffered; that was all.

Dad was sent from California to an institution in Kansas, where his belt and shoelaces were taken from him and he was poked and prodded by a legion of mental health practitioners. The family had very little contact with him. I can only imagine how bleak life must have looked to him. Surely his career and calling as a minister were over. That was his love! That was his life! Surely he would always ever after feel like a ghost, holding on to his secret scandal. Surely he would never again be happy and confident.

After several weeks, Dad was permitted to go home and enter a nearby clinic. Soon, he was able to drive himself there, spending all day every day in group and individual therapy. By the time I got home from school for a summer job, he seemed subdued but normal. He talked about his therapy and his therapist a lot. That was my dad: always obsessively fascinated by whatever he was discovering. He discovered psychotherapy and soon wanted to talk, constantly, about learning to express your feelings. I listened warily.

Back at school for my senior year, I heard with mixed feelings that my parents were moving to Kansas. My dad had been called to a church in a small town, which I thought (and I suspect he did too) was the equivalent of putting the old gray mare out to pasture.

Now, many years later, I have a very different perspective. That Kansas church took in my parents and appreciated them for just what they were. The church's warmth and quiet pride in their pastor was a healing lotion for both my parents. They had some very happy years there, and my dad was thoroughly restored. For some time, he remained enthusiastically obsessed with psychotherapy and would tell you all about it. That wasn't a bad bargain. We learned to talk about our feelings. We became a closer and warmer family.

What had come to me in the guise of a bitter end turned out to be a transition.

My parents had felt abandoned and bereft, tossed on the trash heap. They were ashamed, frightened, and humiliated. They discovered, in the bleak Arctic of their loss, that some people won't let go so easily. They still had friends; not everybody was too embarrassed to talk to them. They also discovered new life and new friends in a new church and a new place, where they would never have gone by choice. They discovered new psychotherapeutic tools that helped them live more openly. It turned out to be a good thing—though not perfect.

It was good for their children, too.

* *

"Life is difficult," as Scott Peck famously wrote in *The Road Less Traveled.* No less true is this: "Life can be shattering." It's one thing to face adversity on your road to success. It's another to fail, utterly and irreversibly—to face mind-buckling loss that you can't get over. That happens in life, though not many people tell you about it when you meet them.

When your life shatters, your only hope is that others will help pick up your pieces. That's one reason to make sure there *are* others in your life: those who will not be embarrassed or put off by your plight. Family, of course. Friends, to a remarkable degree. Church members, sometimes. Neighbors, often, but probably not if they don't really know you more than to wave at you on the street.

God, always. You need God when you are shattered. To be more specific: you need Jesus, the God who has suffered, who has been shattered.

What can we make of the Bible's long, detailed account of David's demise? Could we conclude that it ended well? That important lessons were learned? Two sons died, a daughter was raped, and the nation and its king suffered incalculable violence and disruption. It is a story without a happy ending and without an obvious rationale for its telling. Maybe David gained from discovering he still had allies in a time of desperate need. Maybe he emerged a stronger leader and a better parent. However, the story in the Bible doesn't say so.

I have heard people interpret these stories seeking wisdom about parenting—concluding that parents should not play favorites and should discipline their children. True as those lessons are, they don't get at the deeper meaning of David's story, which surely centers on the way in which regret and guilt clouded his vision. He failed as a parent and as a king because he failed as a man.

If David was depressed and didn't want to go to work, he is not the first or the last to feel that way. A letdown after great effort and great success is very human. In that letdown, however, David faced a moment of testing. Bored and perhaps depressed, he saw a beautiful woman and tried to self-medicate with sex. From there, a cascade of decisions led to murder, and from murder to moral paralysis, and from paralysis to self-pity and almost to the destruction of his kingdom. It was a long downhill trip to hell on Earth. He was shattered.

This is distinct from the loss he experienced in Ziklag. There, David suffered through no fault of his own: he was a victim of circumstances, trying to somehow find a way through. Now, in Jerusalem, he suffered shattering loss through his own fault. He brought it all on himself. That is a far worse, far more debilitating loss.

There's this, too: Before Ziklag, David had never really had much to lose. Almost from the time he killed Goliath, he had been running from Saul. But now, running from his son, David lost a kingdom. He was on top of the world and surely thought he could never lose. When you fall so far, it's especially hard to believe it has happened. It's especially hard to get up again.

I've tried to draw out qualities that link David to David's Son Jesus. Here, however, there do not seem to be any. David's problems of sin and regret and paralysis, his failings as a father were not Jesus'.

Only one aspect does link the two men: their procession out of Jerusalem, weeping, barefoot, taunted, cursed. That procession is an emblem of the sorrow of our world.

In both cases, the problem of sorrows was rooted in the problem of sin. Sin caused David's self-destruction and deterioration—his own sin. Sin also caused Jesus's destruction—*our* sin. He carried the sins of humankind. Jesus as well as David might well have said: "If only I could die instead of you."

Jesus did.

QUESTION FOR REFLECTION

What is the worst thing that ever happened to you or your family?
How does it affect you?

12. RESTORATION

In 1940, Thomas Wolfe's posthumous novel, *You Can't Go Home Again*, was published. The plot describes an author who publishes a novel about his hometown, only to discover that his depiction has enraged the townspeople and he isn't welcome back. The title has taken on a wider and deeper meaning: the idea that nostalgic memories of childhood can never be matched by adult realities. Going home is always disappointing. You can't recapture the past.

David's career closes on this note. His golden era is gone. He began as a youthful hero, striking down Goliath and then leading troops in battle to save their nation. But beginning with Bathsheba, he fell into a dark cave stinking with guilt and death. He wandered, blind, until he encountered the worst enemy of all—his own murderous son, Absalom.

David could not pull himself out of this hole. He would have died in it—and he almost did—but was saved by his army. When many deserted him, his soldiers stuck. They fought the battle to overcome Absalom.

Now David wants to go home. He wants to recover from his losses and restore his kingdom. What that means, in the 2 *Samuel* account, has little to do with the place called Jerusalem. His homecoming is described almost entirely through relationships. It reveals David interacting with those who opposed him and cursed him, with those who stuck with him all the way, and with some who were simply caught up in the tide of war through no fault of their own.

David will live on as king for many years, and Israel will thrive. David will die of old age in his own bed, passing a prosperous kingdom on to his son Solomon. He will be remembered as the greatest of kings, and for good reason: he did what kings are meant to do, defending the nation's sovereignty and carving out its identity. Through his psalms, David passed on an indelible legacy of passionate, personal faith, which became central to Israel's self-identity.

The historian who wrote 1 & 2 *Samuel* wants us to focus on something different from that memory of the good and great David, however. He wants us to understand how deep the cost David paid for his sin, and how shaky was his restoration. He does so by bringing out a parade of people to see how David deals with them—to see whether he can ever really go home.

* *

David's recovery begins with his review of troops after their victory. David feels his way, moving tentatively, almost seeming to have forgotten how to be king. He is trying to regain what was once so natural and fluid.

Joab, rude and rough, tells him to stop sobbing over the death of Absalom, to get on his feet and go out to encourage the troops. Otherwise, he threatens, they will desert you, because you treat them like trash.

It's easy to dislike Joab, because he's brash and rash and violent. He's on David's side, but not of David's persuasion. As Eugene Peterson writes, "Joab…is the prototypical strong man. He kills first and thinks later." (*Leap Over a Wall*, p. 126) In an action movie, Joab would be the rough dude you can't really trust even though he's on your team.

Yet in this case, Joab is exactly right. A leader can't moan about his sorrows and ignore people who risked their lives for him.

David manages to stir himself. He gets up and goes out but finds no words of encouragement to offer. He sits silently in the gate while the troops pass in review. He is utterly passive. The soldiers walk by in silence, afraid to cheer. David has found strength to make a slight gesture, but he is nothing like the young commander who once led his band of warriors against the Philistines.

It's a critical moment. The nation is arguing with itself. The majority of the people, it appears, wanted to trade David for Absalom. Now that Absalom is dead, they are not sure what to do: invite David back? Or look for another leader? David's passivity and fear have shaken their allegiance. For years, he's hardly been a king. He ran away from Absalom. Can they put confidence in him again?

David knows this argument is going on. He must, he knows, help them to answer the question in his favor. His first action is to send a message to Jerusalem, to two priests who remained loyal when he fled the city. The priests served as David's eyes and ears, secretly sending messages of Absalom's plans. They did so at great danger to themselves and their families.

David appeals to the priests. He wants them to help unify his tribe of Judah behind him. He is building support, beginning with his base.

David also makes an extraordinary gesture: he sends a message to Absalom's general, Amasa, offering him the top army post, replacing Joab. Here, too, he appeals to tribal solidarity: "Are you not my own flesh and blood?"

Joab is David's flesh and blood, too, but David is angry with Joab. He cannot forget that Joab killed his son after being ordered to treat him gently. Time and again Joab has proven himself to be a violent, bloody man. David miscalculates badly, thinking that he can replace Joab. As soon as Joab gets the opportunity, he will stick a knife in Amasa.

For the present, however, David's appeal to his tribal base is effective. He has not lost his political touch. Judah is won over, and they invite David to return to Jerusalem.

Furthermore, the other tribes now feel pressure not to be left behind. When David arrives at the Jordan River, escorted by his relatives, other tribes begin to come and make their appeal. First in line is the extraordinary Shimei, the man who hated David so deeply that at the risk of his life, he followed him in his retreat, throwing rocks and cursing at him. Now he rushes to the river and throws himself at David's feet. He makes no excuses for what he did. He simply appeals for mercy. Joab's brother wants to kill him on the spot, but David says no. "Should anyone be put to death in Israel today? Don't I know that today I am king over Israel?" David has not forgotten magnanimity: "All for one, and one for all."

So far, David has managed his recovery well. He has persuaded his own tribe that he is their faithful leader; and he has convinced the northerners that they need to get back into his graces while they can.

Just when we begin to think that David is arriving safely home, Jonathan's crippled son Mephibosheth appears. He looks a mess: dirty hair untrimmed, toenails long and ragged. He says he has been mourning over David, contrary to the accusations that his servant made during David's retreat. The servant claimed that Mephibosheth had stayed in Jerusalem primping himself, ready to be crowned king. Now Mephibosheth puts the lie to that. He accuses his servant of rushing off and leaving him, a disabled person, without means of transport.

David doesn't know who to believe or how to respond. On his retreat, he believed the servant's story, granting him all Mephibosheth's property. Now he half-rescinds that, telling the two to split the family land. This may seem like Solomon's famous decision to split the baby, but in practice, it is not likely to leave anything but festering resentment between the two. They will spend the rest of their lives glowering over the boundary line of their divided farm.

David gets to Jerusalem and confronts the ten concubines he left behind. When he fled, his panicky plan was for the concubines to "take care of the palace." Absalom "took care" of them—putting a canopy on top of the palace and making a public show of sleeping with each one. It was a political statement as much as a sexual one—a middle finger to his father.

Now, what to do? David locks up the concubines for the rest of their lives; they are to be kept as prisoners. He will never see them again, and he will not set them free to start a new life. David put them in a compromised situation, but they pay the price. No grace here.

Doesn't David grasp how much grace God has extended to him? Doesn't he know that those to whom grace is given must also show grace? Why does he treat these helpless and abused women like criminals? He acts like a gracious king while reconciling with his enemies, but with these exploited women, his heart remains poisonous.

It turns out that despite David's politicking, he has not settled the argument within Israel. The ten northern tribes resent being (as they think) second-class citizens behind Judah, David's tribe. A troublemaker named Sheba calls everybody from the northern tribes to desert David and follow him. They all do. This is the ultimate sign of David's unsatisfactory homecoming. His career as king has been devoted to unifying Israel. Clearly, he has failed.

No more gentle persuasion. David sends out his forces to track down Sheba. They catch him in a walled city, where Joab (having murdered

Amasa and seized back his old job leading the army) negotiates with a woman elder to have Sheba's head tossed over the wall. The insurrection is ended, brutally.

David's side wins the battle, but not the war. The northerners' resentment does not go away. Decades later, the division will blow up permanently, and the kingdom of Israel will break apart.

* *

By contrast with David's restoration, consider Jesus. How could he reconcile with those who had deserted him and denied him, allowing him to die friendless and alone? The answer comes near the end of the gospel of John, when Jesus joins his disciples as they return to fishing. He eats breakfast with them and then takes Peter for a walk. "Peter, do you love me?" Jesus asks three times.

Each time, Peter answers with increasing agitation, "Of course I do."

Then Jesus gives his command: "Feed my sheep." (John 21:15–17)

Jesus does not demand that Peter swear allegiance again. He does not make Peter grovel. He simply asks Peter to serve others—to do the work of a shepherd. It is a gracious reply that focuses not on conserving Jesus' power and authority, but on care for others. When you contrast that with David's homecoming, you can't help seeing how much David falls short.

And yet—and yet—David's story is certainly God's story. God chooses him, God enables him, God forms him, protects him, gives him friends and allies, crowns him king—all without appearing. And in David's great downfall, God is also present, judging him, punishing him, and ultimately preserving him. We think we control the narrative of our lives. But another storyteller molds our story into his. David's story is nested in Israel's story, which is nested in Jesus' story, which is God's story of the whole world, including every one of us. We live our lives nested in God's story. He is the storyteller.

This doesn't mean that we are helpless creatures of fate. It means that we make our choices within a much larger, invisible context. We can embrace God's story, or we can try to squirm our way out of it.

David is now back home in Jerusalem. He is king again. Yet he is surely a sadder king than the exuberant young man who danced in the

Spirit when he was chosen. His first wife is estranged from him. His concubines are locked up on the property. Two of his sons are dead, his daughter a victim without any future. He presides over a seething resentment between the tribes.

Perhaps this is the period of his life when he publishes his poems, enabling Israel to incorporate a rich library of songs into their worship. However, it must be difficult for him to read some of his own words protesting his innocence. The *Samuel* historian is certainly aware of this, but nevertheless, he includes Psalm 18 in his text, which includes these words: "The Lord has dealt with me according to my righteousness; according to the cleanness of my hands he has rewarded me." (2 Samuel 22:21)

* *

When we are young, we dream of success—success in love, in work, in family, in fame, and in fortune. As our lives play out, they prove to be a mixture of triumphs and disappointments. We may defeat giants as David did, but we also (like David) make enemies. People love us, but we wander in the wilderness. We set out to host a family Thanksgiving and instead end up with family members who won't speak to each other. Perhaps we are shattered, falling into darkness where temptation and sin capture us, and only by God's grace are we set free.

The Bible speaks of a great judgment, when our lives will be totaled up and assessed. Jesus describes it as a scene before the King, when sheep and goats will be separated based on their treatment of needy people. Long before that day, however, we begin the process of judging ourselves. We look back on our experiences and we remember people—those who scorned us, and those who loved us. We try to make sense of what happened.

The vast majority of our accomplishments grow pale with age. Winning that award? Graduating from that school? Starting that business? If anybody cares at all, it's because they care about us. The sand castles we built will wash out to sea, and nobody but us will mind.

In my later years, such thoughts come often. I haven't quit trying to make a difference in my world, but I am fairly sure that most of my mark is already made. As with David's homecoming, it's a mixed picture. I'm very proud and thankful for some of it. My family, for example: a wonderful wife, and three children who love me and have families of their own, and six grandchildren (so far) who bring extraordinary joy to me. I love my church and I'm thankful for the role I've been able to have in it.

On the other hand, many of my achievements seem to vanish like the morning fog. For decades, I was best known for a magazine column aimed at high school students, "Love, Sex and the Whole Person." It presented a traditional Christian view of sexuality, and I had many avid readers. Now, few remember, and those columns seem sadly out of date. So much in our culture has changed—gender fluidity, gay marriage, "friends with benefits," "living together." What seemed cutting-edge advice now reads like faded newspaper clippings.

David's greatest accomplishment was his royal reign over a unified nation dedicated to God. That would prove very short-lived. Under the kings who succeeded him—even his own son Solomon—God was mainly forgotten. The kingdom broke apart.

On the other hand, David's musical and poetic talents probably seemed more like a hobby than a career. That legacy turned out to be more significant than any of his official business. His psalms have lived 3,000 years, and they live still.

God has his own way of telling stories—a way that takes the smallest things and turns them into glory.

* *

Jesus, in the final week of his career, pauses to look over Jerusalem and sum up. His response? He weeps. "Jerusalem, Jerusalem, you who kill the prophets and stone those sent to you, how often I have longed to gather your children together, as a hen gathers her chicks under her wings, and you were not willing. Look, your house is left to you desolate. For I tell you, you will not see me again until you say, 'Blessed is he who comes in the name of the Lord.'" (Matthew 23:37–39)

That's the cry of a king. He seeks to bring peace, but he can see war coming. He longs to gather Israel's people and protect them, but he knows he is about to be killed and the nation left desolate. He is a young man whose offer of salvation is rejected in the most violent way possible: they are going to execute him.

Like David, Jesus dreams of so much good, and his work turns out muddled and misunderstood. Even his friends desert him. They don't understand what he is trying to do. Jesus must follow his calling to the end. He must give his life to it. But what good can he do after he is dead?

He can rise.

Resurrection is the only answer: new life, new creation. This is exactly why David's story must nest in Jesus' story. If it is merely David's story—if David is only a role model, a hero with courage and faith to emulate, a founder of the nation of Israel—then the story doesn't end well. David's only hope is to rise again.

David knew this—perhaps dimly, seeing the truth in fragments. He knew there was more to the story.

> My heart is glad and my tongue rejoices;
>   my body also will rest secure,
> because you will not abandon me to the realm of the dead,
>   nor will you let your faithful one see decay.
> You make known to me the path of life;
>   you will fill me with joy in your presence,
>   with eternal pleasures at your right hand. (Psalm 16:9–11)

After his terrible fall from grace, David could manage the politics of the situation, using a combination of gracious words and military force to stay in office. There would be no more dancing with the ark, however. He could expect no more jubilation. David had to turn his hopes forward, to Jesus—Jesus, whose name he did not know, but whom he hoped for. Jesus, his own son, who would be the first to rise from the dead—the first, but not the last.

QUESTION FOR MEDITATION

How would you sum up your life?

How would you *like* to sum up your life?

13. DAVID IS DYING

I have a lot of older friends. I meet them mainly through my church, and I take pleasure in their company. They often have an enlarged picture of the world. They seem more relaxed about the mini-crises of church, or politics, or traffic. Many of my older friends possess a sense of humor that helps them manage obstacles. And some of them are very wise.

No amount of perspective obscures the powerful drag of aging, however. Though each one ages in their own way and at their own rate, the tide is going out, and all of them are being pulled in deeper. Health crises become more frequent. Memory slips. Walking becomes more precarious, and the risk of falling grows. People can't do as much, and before you know it, they can't do a lot of things. Getting off the sofa becomes arduous. They lose their taste for food, their sense of hearing, their eyesight. This can be hard to watch. Even harder to endure.

I'm thinking of a couple I know well and love dearly, now living in an assisted living complex. They are some of the most admirable and lovely people I know. Neither of them can drive anymore, which means they need help to get to church or to their doctors (whom they see frequently). She's struggling with anxiety. He's having trouble walking, even with a walker, and he has to use a bag to capture his urine—a bag that often seems to leak. They are brave, strong people, and they love each other deeply. But every year, life seems to get more difficult. As their son told me—he's deeply and lovingly involved in their care—"They have just lived too long!"

The path of success and failure leads here, ultimately. We'd like to age gracefully, but it's not in our control. We always end up dying, no matter how hard we try.

So it is with David, the wily desert warrior, the regal king. In the end, his greatest challenge is that he can't stay warm. His servants pile blankets on his bed, but he still shivers.

The solution is to recruit a beautiful young virgin to share his bed—ostensibly as a human warming pad, but undoubtedly also with the thought that a little sexual stimulation might wake up the old man. Otherwise, why search for a beauty, as they do?

The Bible makes the point that David never has sex with her. Is that a report on his virtue or on his loss of vigor? Probably the latter. She does become his nurse. In the biblical account, she never says a word, but she is always present.

David is weak. Evidently he can't get out of bed. Nobody can effectively lead a nation from bed, especially if he is trembling with cold. His oldest living son, born of the same woman who gave birth to Absalom, takes it in his head to seize power. Somebody needs to run the family business, and obviously Dad can't! Number One Son confers with General Joab and the high priest and arranges a coronation ceremony for himself a couple of miles outside the Jerusalem walls.

This son is a younger version of Absalom, very full of himself and fond of zipping around Jerusalem in a chariot with 50 men running in front. He may not have Absalom's political gifts, however, because in the pinch, his support vanishes. As soon as Bathsheba catches wind of his plan, she goes to David, who may be enfeebled but hasn't lost his sense of power. He immediately counters by having Solomon, Bathsheba's son, crowned. That proves a popular move. With the crowds backing Solomon, Number One Son quickly gives up the fight, begs for mercy, and promises to serve Solomon.

Now Solomon runs the government, and David can be left in peace.

After some time, David recognizes that he is near death and calls in Solomon for some final words. I imagine Solomon leaning over his father's bed, straining to hear the weakened voice. What great wisdom will come from the king's mouth?

David begins conventionally, telling Solomon to be strong, and be a man. He says a few words about following God and obeying his commandments. Then he launches into what he really wants to say.

He starts with Joab. His entire career, Joab has been by his side, and sticking into his side like a thorn. He tried to fire Joab once. That lasted about 24 hours. Joab led the army and David couldn't get along without him. He has resented this for years, but he felt helpless to do anything about it. With a gleam in his eye, he appoints Solomon to do what he could not. "Be smart," he says, "and be careful. But don't let that old SOB die in peace."

Then Shimei. David reminds Solomon that Shimei cursed him on the worst day of his life—when he was running from Absalom. True, he forgave Shimei while returning to Jerusalem after Absalom's defeat. David took an oath before the Lord not to put Shimei to death. Solomon, however, has not taken that oath. "You're a smart man," David says. "You'll know what to do and how to do it. Just make sure he dies wallowing in his own blood."

Those are David's final recorded words, like a scene out of *The Godfather*. What a contrast to David's Son Jesus, who died saying, "Father, forgive them, for they know not what they do."

Think how you would write this scene. David should die reciting, "The Lord is my Shepherd," with all his children and grandchildren gathered at his bedside.

In due time, after David dies and is buried, Solomon follows his father's last wishes. When Number One Son asks to marry David's beautiful bed companion and nurse, Solomon has Number One Son executed. Seeing what is coming down, Joab flees to the Tabernacle and grabs the horns of the altar, thinking that its sanctity will protect him. Solomon orders him killed anyway.

Solomon bides his time with Shimei, but when Shimei breaks the rules of his house arrest, Solomon calls him into court and has him stabbed to death in front of everybody. Like a good Mafia son, Solomon does exactly what his father requested.

* *

David's dying words throw questions in our face. Chief among them: Why is this here? Why did the historian choose to finish David's life on this note?

He could have skipped it. He skipped a lot of other events of David's life. This final scene could be left out, the way we often edit people's lives at memorial services—especially if they get cranky or mean in their final years.

Unmistakably, this final stomach-turning scene of David's life is included for a reason. But what is that reason?

I believe the author of the *Samuel-Kings* history is sending us a message: "Don't idolize David."

Human beings are naturally hero worshippers. We idolize athletes, movie stars, musicians, billionaires, politicians, and pastors. Among them are many fine people. But in their lives, we can also locate cheating, lying, adultery, greed, abuse, the whole list of deadly sins. The author of *Samuel-Kings* would tell us: you know far too much to think that David was an ideal man. His imperfections never got worked out. He carried them to the grave.

As Jesus tells us, "Only God is good." David is not God. You should worship God only.

The story of David's life gives us ample reason to worship God. God used David to save Israel from destruction. God used him to establish Jerusalem, and to bring the ark there. David became a pattern of the good king, the Messiah, not because he was a sterling character but because God gave him victory over the Philistines and preserved his life when he ought to have died. God did it!

This is very clearly the message of Psalm 89, which focuses on David and his impact:

> Once you spoke in a vision,
>   to your faithful people you said:
> "I have bestowed strength on a warrior;
>   I have raised up a young man from among the people.
> I have found David my servant;
>   with my sacred oil I have anointed him...
> He will call out to me, 'You are my Father,
>   my God, the Rock my Savior.'
> And I will appoint him to be my firstborn,
>   the most exalted of the kings of the earth.
> I will maintain my love to him forever,
>   and my covenant with him will never fail.
> I will establish his line forever,
>   his throne as long as the heavens endure."
> (Psalm 89:19, 20, 26–29)

Everything mentioned in that psalm is God. What is David credited for? He responded. He acknowledged God as, "My Father, my God, the Rock my Savior." (This he certainly did, in psalm after psalm.) Nothing is said about David's great personal qualities. The psalm doesn't address his good looks, his leadership, his passionate nature. It just says, "I found him. I raised him up. I gave him strength. I anointed him." The story of David is about God.

Someone may object, "Didn't God say that David was a man after God's own heart? And doesn't that imply that David had special qualities?"

Two places in the Bible mention David as being "after God's own heart," one in the Old Testament and one in the New. "You have done a foolish thing," Samuel said to Saul when condemning him. "You have not kept the command the LORD your God gave you; if you had, he would have established your kingdom over Israel for all time. But now your kingdom will not endure; *the* LORD *has sought out a man after his own heart and appointed him ruler* of his people, because you have not kept the LORD's command." (1 Samuel 13:13, 14, italics added)

The apostle Paul refers to this in a sermon: "After removing Saul, he made David their king. God testified concerning him: 'I have found David son of Jesse, *a man after my own heart*; he will do everything I want him to do.'" (Acts 13:22, italics added)

Both passages emphasize obedience as the special quality God sought. David obeyed—at least he did most of the time, when he was not scared out of his mind, depressed, or about to die. David did truly love God and longed for his kingdom to flourish. For David, life wasn't all about David.

So what exactly does it mean, "a man after God's own heart?" We are talking about God's heart, not David's. David was formed by God's heart. He "took after" it. He had a piece of it. Thus, he called out to God as "my Father, my God, the Rock my Savior."

Yet for all that God's heart did to shape him, David was a royal mixture. That's the evidence of the story, as told in the Bible. He had great moments. He had ugly moments. And he ended his life in pure nastiness.

I think that says to you and me: don't give up on God, no matter what happens. He is telling a story that is bigger than your story, much bigger and much better—and he wants to nest your life in it.

Let's say, too, in reflecting on the ugly end to David's life: dying is hard. It's so easy to get petty when you are scared. It's so easy to be mean when you are in pain. It's so easy to lie when your family members are asking questions that you don't want to answer. It's so easy to be greedy when you are about to lose everything.

David's heart was not like God's heart as his death drew near. His pent-up anger and self-pity erupted and he arranged for vengeance. Didn't he have better things to think about as he prepared for the end? He did, but he didn't.

That said, let's give David a break. God did.

* *

If David was such an imperfect man, what do we learn from him? Why does the Bible devote so much space to his life? Why did his reputation roll down the centuries?

Two reasons: David is us. He is exactly the kind of person I am, only more so. He lived out all I wish to be and all I fear to become. When we study David, we have opportunity to see ourselves. It is as though God drew us with bright colors, ten feet tall. In David, we can see and ponder our lives on the path of success and failure. I've tried to nudge those reflections in this book.

Second: God used him. His reputation endured because Israel endured. He set the kingdom on its way and it carried on—a people used by God to transform the world, despite failing as much as or more than David.

Why do we study Winston Churchill? Why do we study Thomas Jefferson? Why do we study Queen Elizabeth? Martin Luther? They all had glaring flaws as well as sterling qualities, but we study them principally because they played crucial roles in history. David did too—in God's history. He is the father of Jesus. He is the template for the Messiah. He ruled the kingdom that never ends. To study David's life is to be awed by the power of God to put a very earthly, very failure-prone human being to use for extraordinary purposes.

David ended his life grinding on memories of being cursed and abused. His thinking was so small! It was all about him! He had other, better thoughts—think of the psalms he wrote—but in the end, they were eclipsed by the venal, the selfish, and the bitter. God help us all! And yet! And yet God is bigger than David's smallness. He is bigger than us, too.

I don't see myself ordering revenge against my enemies, but who can plumb the depths of their own heart? Apply enough pressure, or pain, or fear, and I don't know what I am capable of.

I can't guarantee how my life will end, but nevertheless, I am sure God will make something out of it. It's his world, he's called me, and I've put my future in his hands. Let Paul's words sum it all up: "So, what do you think? With God on our side like this, how can we lose? If God didn't hesitate to put everything on the line for us, embracing our condition and exposing himself to the worst by sending his own Son, is there anything else he wouldn't gladly and freely do for us? And who would dare tangle with God by messing with one of God's chosen? Who would dare even to point a finger?" (Romans 8:31–33, The Message)

We have a drive to succeed, and that's a good thing. It motivates us to work, to persist, to dare, to dream, even to pray. Human beings have awesome powers of creativity, and our ambitions push us forward with these. Without ambition, there would be little science, little art, little building, little invention. The world would be a poorer place.

Yet as we have seen in the life of David, the way forward is treacherous. We must—*must*—put our ambitions in God's hands. We must ask him to overrule our faults. We must ask him to make beauty out of the flawed material we bring him. He is the Lord of Success and Failure.

QUESTION FOR MEDITATION

What must you do so you won't end your life on a sour, vindictive note?

END

ACKNOWLEDGEMENTS

As always, I rely on my friends to help me by reading and commenting on the manuscript. This book has been an unusually long time in the making so I may have forgotten some who did so. I'm very sorry if I did! These are for sure: my wife Popie, always my best and most tireless reader; Philip Yancey; Dan Baumgartner; Fred Prudek; Joyce Denham; Haron Wachira; Scott and Jill Bolinder; and Jeff Crosby.

What would I do without you?